Praise for **B**
and *Th*

MW01253532

"*The Road We Take* is both evocative and relatable, a collection of poems that inspires the reader to reflect upon their own life—and to wish they could express themselves as eloquently as Barry Lee Swanson. Representing five decades of Swanson's life, this contemplative and life-affirming collection offers something for everyone."

—KATHLEEN BARBER,
author of *Truth Be Told* (now an Apple + TV series) and *Follow Me*

"Barry Swanson's selected poems, spanning over five decades of his life, succeed in revealing his gift to emerge meaning without shrouding it.

His poems range from heartfelt observances of everyday life: 'Part of the old neighborhood is gone. Pulverized by a concrete ball,' to his delight in describing the natural world: 'Brisk mornings, windshield freezes, suntans fade into past tense.'

Some of his poems strike with a distrustful curtness—bloodshot eyes, a sail-less boat on an endless stream, the deaths of Dr. King and Robert Kennedy.

We find reflections about coming-of-age, the tragedy of war, insights about family, marriage, and meditations in memoriam of loved ones, including his restrained but poignant lament, appreciating his father, 'We played catch once—no *Field of Dreams*. And yet, you were, and still are, my hero.'

The Road We Take is a deeply moving lyrical mosaic."

—PHILLIP SHABAZZ author of *When the Grass was Blue: Growing up in the South, Freestyle and Visitation,* and *Flames in the Fire: Poems*

"From his dawning at 'The Age of Aquarius' to his 'Run to the Future,' Barry Lee Swanson's brawny poetic memoir reminds us of days and deeds long gone along the road we take, or perhaps do not take. His heartfelt and soulful verses unravel across the page and thread their way through more than fifty years of living, loving, laughing, and dying. In the end, he lets us know that those who touched us most along the way dwell with us 'In Memoriam.'"

—LUTHER KIRK,
author of *Appalachian Woman* and *Child of Appalachia*

"*The Road We Take* is a work of hope, grief, and triumph. I traveled with it, peeking in on the experiences of the poet's lifetime and in many ways, ended up encountering my own in return. Barry Lee Swanson's language is accessible and vivid. A joy to read."

—CYN KITCHEN,
author of *Ten Tongues* and *Broken Hallelujah*

"*The Road We Take* is filled with poems that are 'confessional . . . indulgent, innocent . . . reflective . . . and sentimental— poems of love, loss, contemplation, and celebration.' Barry Lee Swanson's poems are foremost from his heart and reveal a personal and sincere life well lived, and as Robert Frost once said: 'And that has made all the difference.'"

—GLEN BROWN

STATESVILLE, NC
boathouseproductionsnc.com
boathouseproductionsnc@gmail.com

Library of Congress Control Number: 2023902523

ISBNs: 978-1-7372855-4-0 (hardcover)
978-1-7372855-5-7 (paperback)
978-1-7372855-6-4 (ebook)

Editing: Carol Killman Rosenberg

Interior & cover design: Gary A. Rosenberg

Front cover art: *The Road* by Lara Swanson Wilson
Back cover art: *Swans in Flight* by Chris Dokolasa

THE ROAD WE TAKE

Selected Poems 1967–2022

With gratitude for your support & friendship during this journey.

BARRY LEE SWANSON

Barry Lee Swanson

Boat House Productions
STATESVILLE, NORTH CAROLINA

*This book is dedicated to anyone who has a dream,
and to those, in particular, who encouraged
me to pursue mine—*

*My parents, my wife, Gail,
our family and dearest friends.*

To all, my deepest gratitude and great love.

"We're after ultimates, but we have to content ourselves
with individual composings in the main."

—SIDNEY COX AUTHOR OF *A SWINGER OF
BIRCHES, A PORTRAIT OF ROBERT FROST*

Contents

THE 2010s: EVERY TEARDROP IS A WATERFALL

THE EARLY 2020s: RUN TO THAT FUTURE

IN MEMORIAM

A Note from the Poet

The poems selected for this book span the past fifty-five years of my life. They are an account of my journey and the roads I have taken. They are confessional, destructive, godless and God-filled, indulgent, innocent, naive, narcissistic, prayerful, reflective, romantic, sacred, and sentimental—poems of love, loss, contemplation, and celebration. There is much joy in these poems; there is also the sadness and grief of losing loved ones. It was an honor to eulogize some of my dearest friends and to mark their passing with a poem. Apart from the In Memoriam section, the poems in the first seven sections of the book reflect chronologically the order when they were first written. Some were later revised.

My daughter, Lara Swanson Wilson, contributed her magnificent painting, *The Road,* which graces the cover of this book. Chris Dokolasa's panoramic painting, *Swans in Flight* adorns the back cover. Gary Rosenberg provided the incredible interior and cover design. Carol Rosenberg provided her always professional editorial acumen to this final product. Thanks to Matthew Swanson for his song, Tim Granet for his haiku, and Ruth Aydt for the poem she wrote to me when she was a ninth grader in my Language Arts class. And, as usual, kudos to my extraordinary wife, Gail, for her keen eye and constructive contributions throughout the process of putting this book together.

The book's division into decades marks the many milestones one passes as she or he ages. The titles for each decade were inspired by a particular song of that era. As I reflected back on what inspired me to compose the poems, I had wonderful moments of laughter and tears.

I did not include all of the poems I have written over the years. Some were entirely too personal, and others, simply, too awful. With the exception of the In Memoriam section, I chose to omit the dedications to the poems written to a specific person. Those individuals know who they are, and I have elected to honor their privacy.

It is a dangerous thing at my age to expose oneself to the degree these poems do. As an author, a poet, or a human being, we try to be honest with ourselves most of the time. I am not proud of every road I took; some of my detours were hurtful to myself and others. It was with a deep sense of regret I wrote about those experiences, but learning from our mistakes is part of being human.

Hopefully, you might find a bit of yourself, of your story, in the words that follow. May these poems help you in some way or another as you travel the roads of your life. If so, the hours spent thinking and writing will have been worth the struggle.

My journey has been neither epic nor Sisyphean. It has been mostly transformative and joyous. I hope the roads you choose to take will be the same.

Barry Lee Swanson

December 2022

The 1960s:
The Age of Aquarius

Linear Expression

A dam breaks.
A line begins.
Flesh, blood,
thought, action.

An alternate line begins,
on the other side.

Aware of its advancement,
I march fearlessly on, experiencing
hate, love,
life!

Blinding lights—stumbling,
ideals—unrealistic,
smell of smells, sight of sights,
retreat, reject surrender.

She arrives.
Flesh, beauty.
Essence
of another life.

Fluid—
they arrive.
Substance.
More lives.

The dam closes.
Dirt falls. Flesh—cold.
Blood in a bottle.
Thought processes cease.

Action
complete.
Lines
meet.

View from a Lit Street Corner

In a streetlight spectrum,
on a rain-covered cobblestone avenue,
I thought about it all—how dumb—
that I never really grew.

Never grew to meet you,
in your palace.
Never stopped searching Wonderland for Alice,
asking myself why you couldn't be true.

With none of the answers,
I glanced casually at the light,
wondered when the dazzling dancers
would embrace my hopeless plight.

Grant me pity, show me the city,
a transparent movie,
Out to the ferry and Miss Liberty.
Back to reality—the streetlight—a time not so groovy.

Rain fell—I stood and wondered.
Me, so stupid, a hopeless blunder.

Gazing—

a streetlight spectrum,
a rain-covered cobblestone avenue,
how dumb,
I never really grew,

but, in retrospect, neither did you.

Brown County

Innocent as a complex leaf,
her stay was long, yet brief.
They passed fences and telephone poles,
as the curtain fell in silence on their separate roles.

She, the queen, he the drone,
existing together, yet always alone.
Passing through Brown County,
the queen discreetly discarded another one.

She remained insecure, though never alone.
A legion of drones flocked to her hive, dismissing her groan.
Clinging to yellowed pages, the queen remained a complex leaf.
Her affairs torrid, yet brief.

Brown County disappeared from his rearview mirror.
Broken-down fences, splintered telephone poles.
Moving on in search of different roles,
memories in his mind, now seared.

He lit his Winston, smoke swirled into darkened night.
She'd wished him well.
He'd turned, not seeing where the leaf finally fell.
How would her story end? What would be her plight?

No longer a broken soul,
he drove his Skylark west seeking still another role.

Moon Gaze

The moon above the clouds,
the streetlight,
the gaze far exceeds the reach.

The goals a man sets
much too high.
Yet,
he must try.

Solid brick street,
crickets rejoice, replete.
Stoic homes,
peaceful, complete.

World in turmoil.
Moments like these,
imagined—
gone forever.

As I shouted in the darkness,
shouted out in vain,
"Aspire!
Aspire to attain!"

A Loving Phase

As you walk without me on this earth,
through leaves, snow, flowers, or sand,
or gaze disenchanted into some open hearth,
think back to the hours we walked hand in hand.

We laughed, talked, loved once long ago.
Time has passed, our paths now void of mirth.
We both made it so,
for whatever that's worth.

As you walk into tomorrow without me,
try to remember yesterday's ecstasy,
moments lost in memory's haze,
countless hours, unshackled, carefree,

swimming untethered in our own personal maze,
our time together, our lost and loving phase.

Palingenesis

Golden sun glistens through green leaves;
the starlit sky motions to cease.
Rushing waves hear wailing grief,
beg them to stop; offer release.

A gray suit leaves an old, moldy whore,
pauses before the open cathedral door
where a priest holds a pitcher waiting to pour
and Adam holds on to the deadliest core.

Gray settles softly upon a soaring steeple.
Mystifying unknowns confound innocent people.
The starlit sky had motioned to cease,
while constituents remain blind to the notion of peace.

Young men died in inexplicable wars,
as gray suits return to old, moldy whores.
Pitchers were broken, Adam swallowed the core,
while mourners stood rigid, closing the door.

The starlit sky had motioned to cease,
dread settles down on dead, browning leaves,
waters run still, bereft in grief,
 golden streets turn red, awash in dark, bloody beef.

The starlit sky had motioned to cease.
Denouements were silent, neither famine nor feast.
Gray suits fell through flame-gutted floors,
war—victorious—peace was no more.

Below, echoed laughter—old, moldy whores,
as the golden sun glistened upon charred, ebony doors.

Star-Dancing

Look beyond the obvious,
extend your reach.
Pirouetting,
ignoring your feelings.

Transparent, blue
I plead for you
to come to me,
open and free.

You—a dancing girl,
me—a writer.
A poem leaks from my pen,
asking where you are, where you've been.

You spin and twirl,
I two-step and twitter.
You in ballet slippers,
me, floating in the stars.

Fading from sight
are all the tomorrows
we never had, being crazy and mad,
laughing in the footlights.

Blind, oblivious
to each other,
passing lonely
through space.

Someday, we might seize our dreams,
those stretched beyond our reach.
Spin with Jupiter and Mars
joyous, carefree—a future to face.

Promises kept, or not.
Ends without means,
feelings extinguished, careless dreams—
completely deserving what we got.

What did we seek?
Out there beyond our reach,
beyond fading stars,
beyond Jupiter and Mars?

You, dancing alone,
me, an ink-stained
poet—tear-drained,
sentenced to roam.

Hymn of the Silent Gray

Shadows fell 'cross white-capped water.
He stared with innocent eyes
heavenward for an unknown father.
The women in black smelled of hidden lies.

Standing before a litter-filled gutter,
he asked the House for blind compassion.
Butterflies passed in spasmodic flutter.
He crossed the muddied stream, seeking undetermined passion.

Reaching the concreted opposite side,
he ascended grooved, wooden stairs.
Morning interrupted—void of sun, sorrow, or cares.
He abandoned silken sheets—the young girl's sigh.

A sail-less boat on an endless stream,
his mind searched on questing a dream.
The bridge offered retreat from the water below.
When the boat sunk, there remained nothing left to row.

Shadows fell 'cross white-capped water.
Staring still, he searched with innocent eyes,
for his unknown father.
Truth—a web of hidden lies.

Stretching 'cross the horizon, the sail descends,
the bridge ends.

Standing in the gutter,
as gray moths flutter;
black-clad women file
past the House—a steaming pile.

Women disrobe—muted sighs,
bridges collapse, moths are burned.
If only he'd known, if only he'd learned—
seen with his innocent eyes.

Subjugated by Emptiness,
he kneels to pray,
lost in a prescient silent gray,
where his lonely plea forever stays.

A Reminiscence

Times were then—
we'd sit around drinking beer,
losing cares with nothing to fear—
except losing them.

We read "Stanyan Street" and listened to the warm,
a warm void of color and form.
Remember the warmth of the summer you shared—
the excitement of the times you unexpectedly dared?

Memories pass through misty eyes,
recollections aren't all bad.
Ivory and diamonds you might recall—
memories. Happy, sad.

Have no regrets, my friend,
life is forever, although some things do end.
Your Dulcinea will appear;
touching her tenderly, you'll call her "Dear."

Jimmy caresses Susie—an overflowing Paper Cup.
Rod comes home to find Sloopy patiently waiting up
in a small room on Stanyan Street.
It will all come back.

The times disguised as love,
the times that meant love,
the times that were love.

Love can still be soft and sweet.

Hymn of Chaos in a Bar Called Chances Are

A million stars 'round the rock whirling,
mortar seals the mouths of time.
Legs embracing, touching, yearning,
flags unfurling,

Time revolves 'round circular, concentric lines,
staying here, passing, returning.
Smoke and stale beer in my nostrils burning,
senses awaken, stimulation, learning.

Vulgar noises
shout inexplicit meaning into meaningless words,
desperate cries, flashing strobe lights—screaming voices
praying, dreaming, destroying, pleading to be heard.

The weed's pungent odor sets the nostrils burning,
awakened senses—was anyone actually learning?

The "man"—deaf and blind—
smells buildings burning.
Four are dead, then more. "Stop the learning!"
"Commies have annexed the students' minds."

"Stop the war!" the children scream.
"Fulfill the ever-promised dream!"
The "man" remains deaf and blind.
Youth search on, trying to find . . .

A million stars 'round the rock whirling,
mortar seals the mouths of time.
Legs embracing, touching, yearning,
flags unfurling.

Time revolves 'round circular, concentric lines,
staying here, passing there, returning
as the cosmos awaits and patiently pines,
anticipating the inexorable explosion of learning.

Memento Vitae (reminders of life)

Someday memories meet in a final handshake
where misplaced dreams merge gracefully
with pleasant recollections.

We dreamed once of cowboys and ranches,
of our tomorrows.
Dreaming, we charged up the hill.

Mimicking heroes, we ran
onto green fields and cinder tracks,
smiling, sweating, swearing, suffering.

Relishing each victory, despising each defeat,
we matured, even as youth excused the boyish foolishness
of riding naked on a tractor through sun-drenched fields.

Midnight streetlights eavesdropped
upon our quiet talk of love,
life, and occasionally—the end.

Games do end, teammates separate.
Even-steven things are disrupted
as little boys and girls grow up.

But memories remain—
tucked safely away,
Undisturbed cells reserved for antiquated good times.

Dreams spin away, hours come and go,
forgotten almost as soon as they pass,
but we remember.

Time passes—and memories, once again, meet
in a final handshake where misplaced dreams
merge gracefully with pleasant recollections.

Even in our elder years, on a peaceful porch
with the midnight streetlights still eavesdropping,
in the midst of a hug and tears,

we won't admit we're saying good-bye for
the last time.

Blank Wall Veteran

Staring at the blank, yellow wall
my eyes begin their inevitable fall.
Love had come to mean white ceilings,
wrangling legs, and misused feelings.

Flowers are being burned on earth,
while Christian's raised eyes are killing the Birth.
You asked, "Where are you going?"
I replied, "To the blank wall." Knowing.

The screen has been shoved between,
through the mesh, it's you I've seen.
I go now, soon to be returning.
Leaving—the grass beneath my feet is burning.

The dusty road—a barren stretch of memory.
Having been forever gone. Do you think of me?
Returning—I choose a different road,
upturned sod—seed unsowed.

You asked, "Where are you going?"
I replied, "To the blank wall." Knowing.
But I didn't know.
Why did I go?

Here I stand—another road.
Weeds blossomed, grass rarely mowed.
Tears absent from your soft, blue eyes,
hardened shut instead—misunderstanding, lies.

My eyes scan the landscape, then fall,
observing ubiquitous, rotted leaves covering
    Tommy's pastel ball.
The epilogue remains incomplete
as I stand weary on mud-caked feet

Before the blank wall—
a surrendered veteran.

Dream of an Elder

In the photograph by her mirror
antique images gradually appear.
The blemished table stands, sturdy—marked by time.
She stares at the circular picture to find

his yellowed portrait within a dusty frame.
She embraced him once, almost his name,
when ribbons of rain fell gently through a misty haze
and flowers bloomed silent in fields where they played.

She reappears there on certain bucolic days—always will.
Yearning to join him—idyllic moments, resting forever still.
Images merge by her stained-glass mirror,
where a love, thought lost, remains—so near.

The 1970s:
We've Only Just Begun

Husbonda Paean

I have seen you real in the early morn,
lying beneath wrinkled flowers,
winking at sunshine in newborn hours.
What would I have done had you not been born?

Imagery of white, pink, and green runs through my mind.
Unscathed by merchant's ware in raw, untarnished candlelight,
I've seen you frightened in the tomb of night.
Forgive me, it's only myself I sometimes cannot find.

I have searched now and then, sometimes asking why.
Being with you seems more complete
than phony smiles or acting sweet.
Our union birthed a beauty unwilling to ever die.

I have seen you real in the early morn.
What would I have done had you not been born?

Morning

Trash cans bang gently waking,
as the soft snow crashes softly calling.
Tender is the white dawning.
You unravel from his gentle warming.

Your lover's breath so unsweet,
beauty does not bequeath itself upon his beleaguered feet.
His bristles rest upon your rosy cheek,
love sublime, so discrete,

so early in the morning.

Pausing before you leave,
you watch him sleep, in dreams replete.
Intellect now at rest,
a giant teddy bear, at best.

You'd rather cuddle at his side,
your dimple shows, your face aglow.
Leaving with a soft good-bye,
you descend stairs into virgin snow,

so early in the morning.

Bicycle Rides

Beginnings are usually innocent enough.
Giggly girls lying in wet grass, watching
basketball games under spotlights,
waiting to be taken on expeditions

in search of hidden treasures
and later—bicycle rides.
Bicycles rides don't decide much,
but sometimes they do start things:

kisses by a moonlit lake
hoping bells will ring,
a little girl's wondering
what tomorrow's puppy love might bring.

Bicycle rides lead to walks 'cross fields of virgin snow,
through brown, strewn leaves to a concrete theater stage
in search of private places
when there's nowhere else to go.

Bicycle rides even ignite fears:
like never again seeing the girl who made you real and fun,
like hearing rain falling gently
upon an umbrella sheltering only one.

Marriage begins with two—you turn still another page.
Memories of lonely nights and a cuddly friend,
whose love, a treasure only you could comprehend.
You grow and finally come of age.

24

The little girl gets off her bicycle and becomes a woman.
Bicycle rides end,
as little boys and girls go pedaling
home alone to remembering.

Bicycles don't talk to each other,
neither do they fall in love,
but people do,
and bicycle rides do start things.

Dialogue on a Veteran's Return

Dammit, George. Sorry I missed the funeral today.

Eternity called him over there.
Always seemed like a senseless war to me anyway.

Times like these make me yearn for the County Fair.

He did come home a hero, though—flag on his box and all.

Cain't understand why this year's corn ain't high.
Oh, by the way, VFW's startin' the stags again this fall.

Mary said she never thought he'd die.

Everything's bloomin' now—sure was a purty spring!

Since he's been gone she just sits beneath the old oak's shade,
holdin' her hand on that cotton dress and lookin' at that ring.

Oh, she'll get over it, George, memories always fade.

My darling daughter lost her husband in a useless war,
efficient and insensitive, death came home to our front door.

Drab Recollection in Olive Green

"Preserve your memories; they're all that's left you."
FROM "BOOKENDS" BY PAUL SIMON

Tomorrow will come, and when it's gone
we'll recall smoke drifting toward sheet metal and picnic benches.
We had no use for medals, only cigars sent in brown-paper
    packages.
our reward was a moment of silence on a hillside,

wondering what it would be like.
Would we be heroes believing it was for the common good?
Or would we be butchers? Kill or be killed.
And none of us were even from Chicago.

Love crossed our minds—a forsaking of violence.
Bodies were meant to lie in beds, not trenches.
We dug ours in sand instead, shooting at paper targets
besieged by honeybees.

Bees were free—no organized formation.
Merely conscripted to defend a hive, not a nation.
We had once defended ourselves,
but, long ago, abandoned that idea.

We sat in bleachers instead, considering our own massacre,
conjuring up reasonable criteria to judge sanity.
We couldn't meet our own standards,
because we were there—regimented masses in sterile, white
    places.

Plastic guns and distant faces help recall fading traces
of dreams and promises made to make the most of our tomorrows,
finding time to release regret, marvel at honeybees
flying over in magnificent chaotic masses.

Makes no difference to them though—
they know where their hive is,
but where is the nation?
Tomorrow has come and gone, and no one seems to know,

as we sit silently collecting
memories like dust—somewhat apropos.

Those Glorious Days of Rationalizations

Exploding M16 shells have a foul, burned sulfur smell.
Audie Murphy didn't wear earplugs on his return from hell.
Insanity comes disguised in forms of uninterrupted moments—
optimistic thoughts of tomorrow in terms other than survival
in the prone, night-fire position.

Mammoth mouths overrun microscopic minds emitting inane
    decrees
intent on developing character, turning boys into fighting men.
We were no longer boys,
nor men like these.

It wasn't the sand path marches, weighted down with backpacks,
compressing our vertebra like a Sisyphean boulder.
It wasn't cinder-based push-ups or standing in the pouring rain,
fearing another outbreak of spinal meningitis.

We understood all of that within its absurd context.

Somewhere in back of a steel potholder, there was a vision
that nearly broke me. An image—
a warm, soft body, perceptive mind.
We settled for glossy photos, wondering if we we'd join Madore's
    fantasy.

Opening tin cans with make-believe can openers, we thought of
    real food,
quiet Sunday nights in a hick Woodford County town,
laughing at Reiff's story of his cat staking out its territory.
We dreamed of them, turning down the covers, curling up with
    dog and cat.

We ate cold spaghetti and Salisbury steak, undressed in the ebony
    light of uncertainty,
and crawled into gritty sleeping bags.
We talked late into the night of more familiar things, attempting to
    forget
rationalizations hinging upon insanity.

When my turn came out on the make-believe perimeter,
I wondered just how long a freakin' hour could be,
wondered when make-believe perimeters
and combat zones would become real.

Wondered how long a day could be,
a week,
a month,
a year?

Wondered how long a lifetime might possibly be.

All Too Soon Enough

So, our child,
you make your entrance on the threshold of your mother's pain.

You exist, growing to become somewhat wise to the ways of the
   world.
Your mother and I love you now for what you are—a small,
   helpless baby.
But time will remedy that,
all too soon enough.

Years will pass quickly, and you will make your own choices,
whether to love or hate,
to injure or heal, to laugh or cry,
to despise or forgive, to remember or forget.

Every turn on life's road will offer its own challenges.
Each decision made will impact who you become.
Many will attempt to instill their values within you,
but you must decide what it is you value.

You'll discover life is unpleasant at times.
It is also wonderful.
You'll experience the joy of learning, the exhilaration of
   individuality,
the happiness and warmth of love, and the chaste beauty of the
   creative moment.

Time flees, things change.
Proposed words of wisdom hinge upon senility.
Things that once seemed good and true
turn nonsensical.

You must decide then upon your own truths,
finding both frustration and fulfillment may confound you
     at times.
Do not despair. Persist
and seize each moment of your joyous existence,

which begins and ends
all too soon enough,

our child!

In Praise of Miracles

Winding through the sinuous stretch of roadway out of Landstuhl,
through Kindsbach and Einsiedlerhof,
I thought how miraculous it all was.
Drops of February's winter rain

were swept aside by rhythmic windshield wipers.
Fiats, VWs, Porches, a few Mercedes trucks
passed in procession.
As I, in awe, made my way home

to a three-story apartment
adjacent to Rodenbach fields, greening and awaiting spring.
Farmers blocked the road in protest,
making the passing to Kaiserslautern difficult,

even more treacherous if you were in a hurry.
Bois and I had traveled that way many times,
never in a rush.
Morning formation wasn't mandatory for us.

We talked briefly of driving to New Jersey
once we returned—
a mere 27 days away.
I remained oblivious, still in wonder at the miracle of birth.

Ascending the steps on that afternoon,
two days past our daughter's birthday,
I laid down on the couch,
confident there would be more rainy afternoon naps,

and more birthdays
for our newborn child.

The Pepto Bismol Room

Summer was leaving,
    and autumn set in,
The long recess was ending
    with an abrupt halt,
And kids no longer littered
    the streets at all hours.
Days were spent in cluttered rooms,
    writing on desks, and passing notes.
Bells separated people,
    and people, and hours went by in a hazy shadow.

Some machines taught or tried to,
    asset of the system's "ethics"
While others rattled off numbers
    at a rate of up to 1,000 per minute.

As the bells continued I entered
    the Pepto Bismol Room.
This room was different,
    there was a person in it.
When you were in this room,
    you felt like someone,
Not just
    "third row, second seat."
We talked about things that had meaning,
    and some of the machines began to look
        a little like people.
In the Pepto Bismol Room, everybody was someone,
    and nobody was no one.
As autumn changed to winter
    and winter faded into spring,

I learned from the person in the Pepto Bismol Room,
    and the machines turned into people also.
Sometime the person in the room turned plastic,
    and fake,
But people too have faults,
    and we are all people.

Now as the long recess
    is beginning again,
And kids litter the streets
    at all hours,
My thanks to the person
    in the Pepto Bismol Room.

by Ruth Aydt

The Silent Place

"... deep inside, in that silent place
Where a child's fears crouch."

Lillian Smith

You have seen me crawl inside myself in silence
turning myself outside in,
smiling or pouting without compliance
falling, getting up, losing, sometimes going on to win.

You have taken me to places and followed me to some,
comforted me when I cried, scolded me when I insisted on being
    bad.
You have known me at my best, in both sadness and in fun.
You taught me a boy must become a man and raise his own family,

see his own children grow, develop, be sad and happy.
In so doing, discover the meaning of good-bye, as you have.

"Good-bye, I'm going out to play."
"Good-bye, I'm going to first grade."
"Good-bye, I'm going to college."
"Good-bye, I'm getting married."
"Good-bye, I'm going off to war."

Every single time a child leaves, a part of the parent goes with
    them.
Parenthood becomes a thousand good-byes.
Inevitably, the child's room, once filled with loud music
Or the tapping of an impatient pencil remains silent.

You know me as I really was—and still do.
What more love and understanding could a son request?

The silent place is deserted now. Seldom do I return for a visit.
But there are times I still crawl up inside myself in silence,
turning myself outside in, smiling or pouting without compliance,
falling, getting up, losing, and sometimes going on to win.

Praying hello follows good-bye.

Part of the Old Neighborhood Is Gone

Part of the old neighborhood is gone.
I was an Army lieutenant there—sometimes an Indian scout.
Driving west on Mary Street, listening to a song,
I looked back south and saw that

part of the old neighborhood is gone.

Pulverized by a concrete ball,
relegating stone and brick walls
to wood and dust—
crushed,

part of the old neighborhood is gone.

The apartment where we slept,
where my sister and I played our games,
suffered through measles, chicken pox, and growing pains—
even dared talk of tomorrows, only dreamt.

Friends gone, too.
We've all moved on to
our own families, unimaginable worlds,
joys and sorrows ceaselessly unfurled.

Through time and space,
if our children were to return to that place
where they grew
would they remember what we knew?

Have their childhood homes become a pile of ancient dust?
Or a simple reminder of what we must
always trust: love endures,
confirms, assures.

Home's a place in the heart,
even when far apart.
Part of the neighborhood may be gone,
but memories drenched in love live on.

Two

Two has arrived,
two kitty cats,
two shoes,
two pigtails.

Like *Sesame Street*, one, two, three, four, five.

Little baby girls grow up,
grow hair, grow tall,
learn to talk,
laugh, walk and run,

and soon they become two.

Two,
when a world
is made of a
puppy named Gus,

and a drawer of toys.
Tall
and small
people—

a world full of love.

That's what we want, most of all,
to give you at two,
and always.

A Care Package

I have a weakness.
I care about you,
even if you don't care about me.
I want you to be a success,

but only for whatever that means to you.
I want you to answer every question,
and to feel good about yourself and your answer.
I want you to smile with satisfaction.

I want you to think of yourself
as someone important,
not just another blue-jeaned girl, third row, third seat,
or long-haired guy, first row, fifth seat.

Teachers have faults, too—weaknesses and problems.
One of our problems is lack of time.
I want to see you, really see you,
and talk with you.

Sometimes it seems
we don't understand each other,
that we have nothing in common,
but we do.

I do have a weakness—
a big one.
I care about you.
I like you.

I am not invincible.
I, too, have faults.
Through it all,
maybe

you can be my friend
and I can be yours.

See ya around.
Don't be afraid of weaknesses
or caring or being human
or having friends.

If I care about you
and you about me
then we care about each other
and, hopefully, about ourselves.

A Walled City

Do you recall the walled city,
whatever it was called,
and the European wind
blowing through your hair?

I do.

I also recall
how much I loved
you then.

Still do.

a poem

my mom made a big misteak yesterday—
she bot me a blu jeen jaket
my pop made a bigger misteak yet
he got laid or is it layed off at the factory
i couldn't get a haircut this weak ether.

its funny how sum of my teachers look at me
oh well im no brain—I guess.

sum guys wanted to be my friends today
i just moved in and was real happy to have sum friends.
They—been forgettin my capitol letters—offered me
some things to get hi on then they just laffed when
I said no.

they—I mean They aint my friends no more
but then nobody is—I guess.

I guess about lots of things now days
I guess cause I dont know nuthin much no more
I put my blu jeen jaket on today
but i didnt want to go to school.
I went cause I didn't have nowhere else to go.

A teacher said hi to me today and he smiled at me
I smiled back and it made me feel kinda good inside.
we wrote sum poems in English class
and we talked about symbulls.

The dude next to me drew a pixture of a finger
he said that was a symbull of something—I guess.

Im not sure what symbulls relly are
but I guess I got the idea
and that's the end of my poem.

p.s. im not sure if I can use a ps in a poem
but I got something else to say.
I cant get rid a my jaket—
It's the only one I got that fits now.

I cant get a haircut ether
Cause we aint hardly got enuff money to by grosheries.
Maybe the biggest misteak mom and dad made
Was forteen years ago—I guess.

but then when I feel good inside
Im glad they made that misteak
Im glad they make all the misteaks they do—
It shows there humen.

Cogitationes in Defecit Referendo
(reflections on a failed referendum)

Our daughter sits quietly waiting
for a time to return.
A time
prior to mistrust.

A time
when we felt alive.
It comes back on occasion:
singing, laughing, weeping, creating—

being whole.

A time
when children
were involved
in something "extra."

We've gone underground now.
Lacking any sort of vision,
a Board imposed its will.
Hollow Men.

Memories fade,
as has the will to resist.
Who has lost?
All of us.

Our daughter sits quietly waiting,
eyes bright with hope,
as we tell her
what we recall.

Silently, she clings to dreams
of what might be—someday.

The Temporariness and Permanence of Things

There is, perhaps, the possibility
you don't understand
the temporariness of things,
nor the permanence.

The world does not
come to an end
when puppy dogs
are sent to farms—

just partially.

When I looked through tears
to try to explain
unexplainable things to you,
like thinking of others,

I wondered how many more times
I would have to "stretch the truth"
for you to make
things better.

It was, perhaps, our first
real communication.
I pray
it's not our last.

But then,
maybe I don't understand
the temporariness of things
nor the permanence.

Fragmentation

"Il faut d'abord durer."
(first, one must last)

FROM A *FAREWELL TO ARMS* BY ERNEST HEMINGWAY

Little girls—little boys—she and he
exist within us, every morning, every day.
Struggling with our hidden individuality,
relinquishing, we allow chosen portions to stay.

Who's turn to wash
the dirty dishes?
Impossible we'd surrender and ever so graciously quash
long-forgotten dreams or hopeful, fanciful wishes.

Descending, a hammer of obligation,
minimizes our existence, our identity.
Its ephemeral ascension
reluctantly accepts life's cyclic reality.

Grief's ignored—awaiting our tomorrows,
sifting through memories replete day by day,
a splendid, complex array
of random joys and sorrows.

Pack away dolls and dreams,
repair worn socks, disheveled seams—
a fragment gone,
but you're not alone.

We exist, persist.
We advance,
resist,
and desist.

Renewal.

While picking up toys,
a smile recollects
thoughts of little girls and boys
in tender retrospect.

Who we are and where we are
are different, not the same.
That was then,
this is now,

and where we are
is where we've chosen to remain.

EEO Epigram

Are you a racist?
Yes, bicycles.

No, I mean are you a bigot?
Sorry, not really, only five-foot, five.

Don't you have a race?
Yes, 200 meters.

Don't you understand?

I'm trying, really I am.
Your language is confusing—incomprehensible!

What?

What?

EEO Epigram II

Colors—
black,
brown,
white.

Snow falls,
melting from white to neutral,
upon black-brown earth.
Growth.

Roots sprout forth
from a purely inferior position—
beneath it all.
Birth.

A process—scientific,
cyclic—
briefly assuring us
of life.

Climate changes.
White snow melts.
Black-brown earth disintegrates.
Frozen, uninhabitable turf.

Darkness.
Neither black nor brown
nor white.
Foolish—nonexistence.

Knight's End

Warriors glistening with sweat
listened to orders.
The redheaded General spoke
of the opponent,

of over- and underestimation,
of victory,
defeat,
hard work.

Tying their shoes, retying them,
straightening their socks,
and tightening drawstrings,
the warriors looked boldly at each other.

The General clapped;
time to enter
the arena.
Brimming with confidence,

shrouded in gold and white,
arrayed with a streak of silver,
multicolored but united,
they emerged from the tunnel.

Dancing girls and human pyramids
begged for a miracle,
shrieking for redemption,
and victory.

There arose a second ovation,
a tumultuous roar, as the Green Knights
entered the battlefield
cloaked in superiority.

Giants threw brownish-orange spheres
down through silken nets, envisioning swift-flanking traps;
well-designed plans concocted by their
bespectacled, mathematically astute Knight General.

Two lines—one green, one gold,
opposed, intent on the destruction of the other,
drove toward respective goals,
throats hoarse, palms red.

Silence—
an anthem.
The armies lined up drowning
in a cacophony of cheers.

The battle for the coveted prize
began with a toss.
Who would survive?
Who would win?

Orbs, elbows, and winged feet flew,
As an epic battle ensued.
Bodies—aching, sweating
faces—tear-stained, finished it.

The Green Knights fought gallantly,
enduring the necessity of an extra period,
only to leave the battlefield
devastated and defeated.

The Silver and Gold rode a wave
of elation to their solitary room.
Amidst hugs and tears
they soaked up the sweet dew of success.

The General entered smiling,
praising the moment, a victory for the ages.
But the next battle loomed;
the war was not over.

The ultimate prize was not won—
yet.

Personal Doorways I

"Your personal doorways know your shadows
and number the times you enter, exit, enter
so often having no lines to say
though you are actor and audience to yourself."

FROM "OLD OSAWATOMIE" BY CARL SANDBURG

It's difficult—
opening the door, but fortunately, it was open when I walked in.
Nine of us sat silent, and then—a Freudian-looking Rogerian
    appeared.
Facades faded. We began to feel.

Paranoia, accusations, insecurities all overcome.
Trivia, laughter,
tears, idle chatter,
ominous silence.

We spoke—of children, husbands, wives, and lovers,
rich aunts, Moroccan marriages, small towns, big towns,
pontoon boats, young and old people living, dying
rhubarb jelly, and God.

Athletes, administrators,
grandfathers and grandmothers,
grand times and bad times.

Fears, rejections, loneliness, hatred, uncertainties, and prejudice—
all topics of conversation.
A ruptured appendix, a nearly fatal box car accident, a trip to
    Michigan,

an unfulfilled professorship, a deceased father,
an obnoxious neighbor, another woman, an unloving father,
a desert romance burned out by the Iowa sun.

Grand times?
Wonderful families, happy reunions, finding faith
in Something, caring about each other and discovering
that love is truly a multifaceted emotion.

For two weeks we walked through
the door to room 112 and closed it.
Once inside, we opened our personal doorways.
We opened our hearts to each other.

And because of that we will never
be quite the same.
Thank you for being special and giving me
the courage to take hold.

Our doorways will close now,
just as the room 112 door.
Like all special friendships,
time and distance take their toll.

We depart for new encounters today,
each on our separate journeys,
discovering a different meaning
for that sometimes awkward, multifaceted word.

So, love to all.
Here's to open doors and hearts.

You, the Athletes

It never really ends.

The beginning—bathed in heat and humidity,
practicing twice a day, sometimes three,
searching for flags to mark your way,
smashing drives off a tee.

Shine your putters, polish your shoes,
adjust your helmet, your padded gear,
leave behind preseason blues,
charge into your season—nothing to fear.

You, the athletes.

Autumn air, muggy or crisp.
Battle begins.
Cheerleaders and fans scream, as they insist:
do your best, whatever it takes to rack up wins.

Birdie putts, one last torturous mile,
X block! Set and spike. Coaches, in sheer delight, smile.
Crack heads, bust tail, preen, being ever cool,
find comfort after a loss on a lonely, locker room stool.

Sorrowful defeat, joyful victory.
It'll all even out, you'll see.
Time wends.
A season ends—another begins.

Indoors—
pools, mats, polished floors.

Dive. Takedown. Grab every loose ball.
Get up, push forward, give it your all.

On to State! (Your dream dismissed—a single, missed free toss),
Today, sweet victory, tomorrow bitter loss.
You bask in triumph, wallow in defeat.
Moments, all, destined to one day meet.

The crocus grants life another shot,
you compete again with all you've got;
A smashing serve, a sizzling sprint, a soaring ball, a speeding
    strike.
In the blink of an eye, our seasons vanish like

the crocus.

As everything does in the midst of this mysterious chaos
we call life,
order emerges,
forging a woman or a man from the foundry of strife.

For if you gave your very best,
made every effort to reach your goals,
then you've passed the ultimate test;
your character forged in a formidable mold.

Depart for tomorrow—sweet and bittersweet,
search for the challenges you'll meet, conquer, and defeat.
Tomorrow will come running, without pause, with countless
    beats,
Stretch out and greet it, you, you, the athletes.

Purpose?

There has been some talk lately about purpose,
an allusion made here and there to meaning.
Upon whose purse do you propose?
Upon whose body do you go leaning?

If the day is bright with new tomorrows
then why do we bother with yesterdays?
What happened to you, all the brilliant Clarence Darrow's
when Blacks were running through the maze?

Was it the beginning of another evolution,
or meekly receding into silent revolution?
Failing to respond to a single, anxious query,
too tired, just lazy, or simply growing weary?

Thoughts of wasted yesterdays
guilt-ridden, bewildered, wandering through a foggy haze,
wondering what went wrong,
where it all has gone.

The purpose.
The meaning.
Still not certain the *it* that once existed
is even worth remembering,

but you are.

Afternoon Snowbank

... And if the snow fell,
frozen in time,
multifarious flakes in my hand
not left to melt, but freeze

and beautify.
Beheld by mystical magic,
manifested eternally,
thought of through all ages,

then the serenity of that moment
would pierce the hollowness,
hallowed by silence and wonder,
crystallizing and magnifying

the magnificence of existence.

We laid there in the snowbank,
making angels and laughed.
Plunging toward an imaginary goal line,
we caught the enchanted flakes in our hands.

You seemed somewhat awed.
The flakes melted and were gone.
But they would be replaced by others
when the snow fell—once again.

O Pal O

What can I say to you, my son, as you approach your second year?
Should I speak of things done or those yet to come?
The ologies and ghouls at this point—unknown monsters.
Athletics are still a joy, the mere throwing and catching of a ball—
      no road of life.

Should I warn you of evil and hatred—prejudice?
Can I possibly explain selfishness and egocentricity
to you, my innocent one?
Why do I pose these questions to you

when I am supposed to know the answers?
The time will come for you, as it did for me,
when you will be convinced you will have
arrived and have all the answers.

I will most likely view you as arrogant then,
because I will be older and have arrived
at all the solutions myself—through rationalizations.
You'll say I don't understand, but I do.

I understand that I want you to like yourself,
that's a gradual and ongoing process.
It will include questioning yourself, your goals, and your motives.
Unfortunately, O Pal O, life isn't all hammers, balls,

and Fisher-Price Little People.
It's big people, powerful people, some who will hurt,
some who will help,
but remember this—

if, through all the struggles, you lose sight
of who you are and where you come from,
I guarantee you will lose yourself.
There are so many mysteries,

but the heart remains constant.
Through learning, growing, playing,
loving, living, and dying,
our love will also remain constant and abiding.

The 1980s:
Don't Stop Believing

Three-Ring Circus and Forgotten Big Wheels

The day will come
when the bikes and Big Wheels
will be put away.
The basement will be tidy.

Clothes will be hung neatly in closets,
peanut butter and jelly stains gone from the carpet,
every toilet flushed.
Chairs used only as chairs,

not spaceships or boats or covered wagons.
Blankets will no longer be draped over boxes
as tents
or hidden caves.

Bats, dolls, and balls—
reserved for occasional visits.
The swing set—
no longer an Olympic site.

Nights, peaceful around here then.
No whining, crying, only our laughter,
remembering,
and wishing we could do it all over again.

Aoristic Accolade

We take our last few, precious trips to Dairy Queen.
Strange-shaped balls begin to float through the air.
Fans soon scream,
even dare to swear.

We'll know where we are, as we fall
down laughing in leaves, cheering our final mowing.
Autumn—ever congenial.
Sorrowful—her arms outstretched as empty limbs, mourning.

She lingers—a few remaining sunshine moments.
Brisk mornings, windshield freezes,
suntans fade into past tense.
Brown foliage descends—inclement breezes.

It's here, no thought, no reason.
It's here, another season.

Shedding Our Inhibitions

If I look into your eyes,
and touch your knees,
place my smile and frown upon my palms,
all the while maintaining my cool and calm,

telling you the truth about lies,
begging and asking you, please,
to go with me always,
will you?

Perhaps the only thing better than loving you,
would be growing old together,
or it might just as well be growing young together.
Kicking the sand, laughing, and praying

that other's coming and going
will be as easy as ours.

Catechism of Chaos

You know, Lord,
when the typewriter and Xerox
are going strong,
and the FM blares disco,

when problems stream through my door,
or we lose a tough one—
game or kid—
I reach in, look back up,

searching for
You
to pull me
through another one.

You often do.
Making "Thank God"
not just
another empty phrase.

The Batesville Casket Co. Truck and Orange A.M. Kisses

Looking outside my office window, I noticed the Batesville
    Casket Co. truck
making its delivery to the funeral home today.
How interesting to be peddling and delivering
that in which so many of us are finally put away.

Harry Chapin wrote a sequel to "Taxi."
Now even he's established.
I suppose we are too, you and me,
no longer wild and blushed.

What if the establishment ceased to exist?
Would the radicals continue to persist?

I don't even know who the radicals are anymore,
or if they even recognize themselves.
Booming sounds blare from four-wheeled cells,
beyond recognition, understanding, or rapport.

We were once there,
believing we knew exactly what we were doing,
Being cool, moving and grooving,
quite a psychedelic pair.

Our lives now consist of dandelion bouquets, violet jelly,
    crayons and coloring books,
early morning Tang stains,
sleepy smiles, and groggy looks,
as daily we witness necessary growing pains.

Off in morning light with orange A.M. kisses I'm sent,
willingly, joining the establishment.
Is it me against whom the radicals rail?
Across the street, mourners sob and wail.

The Batesville truck moves on, lonely, moribund at end of day,
ornate wooden boxes remain, reminding us where death resides.
A pall wrapped in silence, the ebbing of all the tides.
Mortality claims victory, imposing its eternal way.

Our time is now as love abides
with bedtime stories and night-night hugs—
little eyes closed in prayer. We tuck those little bugs into snugly
    rugs,
as eventide subsides.

No solitary taxi ride tonight, for I am not alone.
This is where I reside—this cherished place, I call home.

The 1990s:
Jump Around

A Prayer for the Youth

Lord—

We've stopped running, pushing, shoving, struggling,
even studying for the moment.
We're taking some time to pause,
reflect, and celebrate!

We ask you bless these young people
in their pursuits.
Grant them vision and courage
in their commitments.

Allow us this one brief moment
of reflection
remembering the courses that have carried
us to this place and time in your endless space.

Take these youth to their respective tomorrows.
protect and care for them.
Assist them in achieving
their distinctive successes.

And be with each of us, this evening, Lord—

Helping us every so often
to stop running, pushing, shoving, struggling,
even studying.
Help us to remember your example.

Help us to remember and give thanks
for our own unique existence
and to give thanks
for that existence having meaning.

Amen

Voices

The windows were open—the heat of summer.
Voices, outside, heard through the screen, above the buzz of bugs.
They sat under the streetlamp post, laughing, dreaming
of places far off and how they could save this sorry world.

The voices carried on through the night,
deafening idealism, persuasive language,
sadly lacking
the certainty of experience.

There was love in those voices,
for one another, or the other,
not present but imagined somewhere in time.
They deposited memories someday remembered.

Those voices come to me now
through my own memories,
spilling out,
lingering for a moment, reflecting an innocent time.

All have been there,
another galaxy where things are
as they're supposed to be,
where hope stretches

like an open highway,
and we hopped in our cars
proceeding due North
toward Truth

to a place
where all dreams

come true.
And when we arrived

voices were there, too,
whispering in the moonlight
under the lamp post,
talking about what had been

and what we wished we'd been.
Through similar screens
our parents listened
to our voices.

The buzz now in our heads
isn't from bugs,
but rather the voice
of deep regret,

of the world we wished for,
the world we imagined.
That world remains
partial—unfinished,

not one of our dreams
but one of reality,
beautiful still but tainted.
Not for them though, not now.

Their voices ring loud, clear,
and true;
a better tomorrow,
as the night lingers on.

All God's Children

You look past our faces,
beyond the dirt, the frown.
You look into our eyes,
deep into our souls.

You aren't afraid to touch us,
hold us,
hug us,
use the "word."

We don't hear much of the "word."
It's not their fault—they don't know how.
You seem to understand our pain,
dry our tears.

work our case,
protect us,
show us what the "word" really means—
every day by the way you treat us,

all of us, who are called
God's children.

A Mother's Love

While their births came on the pangs of pain,
amidst the water and the blood,
through the forceps and the tears,
Love was there.

While peering through proud and glistened eyes,
watching the pageant's ragamuffin soloist,
celebrating His birth,
Love was there.

While holding the crying, bloodied child,
comforting each one,
telling them it would be all right,
Love was there.

While sitting on a thousand bleacher seats,
yelling support,
encouraging, never accepting flimsy excuses,
Love was there.

While waiting patiently in a hospital waiting room,
praying for healing,
fearing the worst,
Love was there.

While celebrating holidays, graduations, championships,
baptisms, confirmations,
while mourning the loss of loved ones,
Love was there.

While kneeling by their bedside,
teaching them about His power and grace,
assuaging their doubts and fears,
Love was there.

While opening presents on Christmas morning,
basking in the love of your family,
to whom you have so consistently and unselfishly given,
Love is here.

Pinions and Pretenses

It's your countenance—
(big word for the look on your face)
that throws people off.
They don't really know what's deep inside.

It doesn't reveal your softness,
or gentleness with pets or young children.
Maybe it's the announcer's voice,
or your obsession with "ball."

They don't hear you singing,
rejoicing in beauty.
No! You're no Beast.
Your *wing* is more angel's than pitcher's.

The Abbot knows, like I do.

When I look into your eyes,
I know who you really are.
We need to look into eyes, not merely at the pretense of a face.
Some might be surprised at what they would see.

Lifted up by the angel's pinions,
they'd see a soft, musical soul
winging its own way to a peaceful place,
graced by the countenance of absolute truth.

Discipline in the Main Office

They advise
to look into your eyes—
one of the symptoms—
bloodshot.

I'd rather look
into your soul
to see
if love dwells there.

Another word
for the Almighty,
the Omnipotent,
the God of all.

Depends on your culture,
doesn't it?

Maybe we'd like to believe
that entity dwells
somewhere
in us.

Giving us compassion,
understanding,
empathy,
honesty.

I try to look
behind your eyes,
searching
for your soul,

for a harmony
that might have a chance
to coexist
within us both.

You, your bloodshot eyes
mine, tear-stained.

Could be
we're seeking the same eternal perspective,
traveling temporarily together,
seeking a forever security

beyond our human comprehension,
beyond the saints and the sinners,
while your tears drop on my desk,
pleading for mercy, for forgiveness.

But the Zero Tolerance rules
expel you from any chance
of redemption—
cast to the streets

with bloodshot eyes,
doing your best to survive.

A Long Line of Lovers

I remember,

though yesterday's been swept away,
stored gently for another day.
I gaze at photos aged and brown,
my bride adorned—an exquisite, sequined gown.

Child-like, we once listened to tales of love and glory,
rapt with each and every story.
They were young then; returned from sea and flight.
Tomorrow's dreams anew in each one's sight.

Years slipped swiftly by.
Lives passed—
a nod, a sigh.
Minutes, hours, days elapsed—so fast.

Romance—so fine.
Precious moments remembered still—
of touch, of warmth, of endless thrill.
Love is constant, patient, kind.

So, stretch toward tomorrow,
its promise burden free,
abandon the regret of things not meant to be.
Embrace each moment, every joy and sorrow.

And may today reflect the best
of a love enduring, forever blessed.

The Little Things In Between

"Neighbors bring food with death and flowers
with sickness and little things in between."
From *To Kill a Mockingbird* by Harper Lee

What is it about giving that makes us feel so good
and receiving that makes us so humble?
The givers bring dishes of food, send cards, or send
    love over the phone,
and expect nothing in return.

How unusual yet how significant,
to be remembered and cared about and cared for.
Meals on wheels—bisque, casseroles, pot pies,
    chicken, pork,
meatballs, stew, lasagna, every dessert imaginable.

And then there's Mom.
She always seems to know how to make us feel good
even in bad times.
Must be a mom thing, like goulash and potato soup.

We dig into treats:
apple pie, apple dumpling, apples and caramel dip,
no sin here.

Caring expressed in so many ways.
Why does it take an illness or a death
to initiate this kind of concern?
Why isn't this an everyday occurrence?

It's like bisque or any of the other wonderful recipes
    that were shared.
The ingredients are always there,
maybe not readily available,
but a shopping spree or a search will uncover them.

Add time and skill,
blend it together
and give our gifts to each other
every, single day.

Do unto others,
love thy neighbor as thyself,
He taught us all that,
but we forget.

It's a lesson we need to remember,
just like we remember our friends
who have given so much,
and to whom we have returned only our thanks.

It's not just the bisque, soups, stews, casseroles,
    cards, flowers, and desserts,
for which we are thankful,
But it's for all the little things in between,
which we simply call love.

Doin' 80 on 88

*"Abundance is . . . ruby taillights and diamond
headlights creating a freeway necklace in the dark."*

—Unknown

Driving down Interstate 88
doing about 80,
the black road and white lines
lay a ribbon to my destination.

Compact discs play
show tunes, songs of Christmas and the sixties.
My mind races aimlessly,
unlike the highway.

Somewhere between DeKalb and Dixon,
on the way to Sterling-Rock Falls and Erie,
rambling and racing,
consciousness flows.

Ulysses returns.
To where—Dublin?
To whom—Helen?
For what—love?

The sun will rise on Thanksgiving Eve.
Cars will pull into eastern ports in Chicago;
others will dock west in Des Moines.

I'll pull into a cement drive
somewhere around dusk,
when streetlights brighten the dwelling where now
    I occasionally reside,
and light breaks forth from inside that house on
    Prairie Street to welcome me.

I miss ordinary times,
moments that swirl through
my mind while cruising at 80
on 88.

Heading home.

In These Moments

There was a time

when a lump was leveled by simply stirring it more.
The mud pie was smoothed out and cut into equal pieces,
the oatmeal was made eatable,
and the gravy was poured over the potatoes and dressing.

A spoon or some stirring utensil
would be used to remove the lump.
By beating the lump repeatedly,
it would blend into the mixture.

The lump almost magically became
a part of the whole.
No longer distinctive in its appearance
or substance.

The word *lump* now means something totally different.
It changed us.
We appreciate our moments together.
We hold on tightly to the present.

The lump has
made us whole.
Beaten around by life,
mixed together with a mystical love,

we have come to more completely understand
the precious value of the moments
we are privileged to share,
the moments we so recklessly take for granted.

The lumps are gone now—yours and mine.
Occasionally, mine reoccurs
in my throat
when I think of you

and thank God
for answered prayers,
and these present times
when love blends us together

like it was
meant to be.

Lamppost Lamentations

Did Frank Sinatra ever stop under
a streetlight, toss his hat aside, light a smoke,
and contemplate who he was?

Did Gene Kelly stop his dance
when the rain ended, put away his umbrella,
and wonder why he existed?

I did—once upon a time,
not in a conjured fairy tale,
but under a streetlight around midnight.

In the sweetness of youth
I stood there and randomly thought—
no hat, no smoke, no umbrella.

There on the bricks,
wondered where I was going—
still do.

Stuck one block north of forever,
dancing and puffing on memories
glad to have had a few moments to think—

just like Frank and Gene.

At Stone Avenue

Arrival

Anticipation awaits at the train station.
There's an "I can't wait" sitting on the bench,
twitching and shuffling.

The photographer sits with his instrument,
which he hopes will etch the antique steam engine
into a frozen frame, a moment remembered again and again.

In the meantime, he focuses on a young black boy.
The shutter snaps on the image of a lollipop being consumed
with the same "I can't wait" anticipation.

A "long hair" sits youthfully smoking his cigarette.
Music pulses through his system, carried by tubes into the
    portals of his ears.
Sipping his coffee, an "I can't wait" taps rhythm in his brain.

A train arrives, but it's not hers.
We sit with anticipation; the photographer, the young boy,
his mother, the aspiring musician,
and me, the writer, scribbling notes about ordinary people
    and love.

I can't wait,
But I do.

When the train, at last, arrives,
it's like seeing her for the first time.
The antique steam engine chugs by the station.

The photographer clicks his machine with precision to assure
    a degree of permanency.

The little boy hugs his father and drops the lollipop on the
    sidewalk,
the musician unhooks to greet his friend.

The moment for me is affixed with a kiss.
We depart from the arrival,
waiting no more.

Departure

Quiet sits with us in the front seat.
It's comfortable, but melancholy.
We open the trunk, removing memories.

Sitting on the bench opposite the station,
we wait together for the westbound
heading for tomorrow

when we will sit alone,
sipping our coffee and looking at photographs.
Music will take us back to the days of children and lollipops,

back to the "I can't wait" moments,
wanting to do it all over again.
And then boarding reality,

left with a longing for the next time,
sitting there with anticipation
and "I can't wait."

Sadness wells in my eyes
with the knowledge that I must.

At the Park

They walk,
(a short walk)
descending the infamous "substitute" stairway,
emerging into the light,
where photosynthesis occurs.

They skip into the park,
the one where basketball courts
meet at the center
and a tower enshrines a not-so-slick slide.

Swings are set—
wide and narrow seats,
accommodating most that wish to fly.
The lucky ones catapult into the sky.

Just as swiftly,
they're returned to the earth of mulch and grass
drenched with dandelions,
hurling flowers' spear-like stems in playful glee.

Children playing,
lost in the moment.
Where do they go,
the children and the moments?

II

Innocence becomes confounded with applications and uncertain
futures,
propelled to God knows where.
A prayer is lifted somewhere that their life support systems are
sufficient
to withstand the reality that saws them into little pieces.

There's a chance they'll be discarded for newer models,
a swing that fits all,
suspending them a little longer in space,
or, maybe, a slide that won't stick.

Perhaps, someone will invent a teeter-totter that's perfectly balanced,
no matter who's on the other end.
Heaven forbid they'll remain in neutral,
grinding up first gear, stuck without wax paper or a push.

Toys will change,
swings may become stationary.
They just wanted to play,
but it's time for the children to go home.

Another walk—
(a short walk)
navigating a new stairway,
emerging into the light,
where photosynthesis occurs,

into the park,
where play never ends.

The 2000s:
A Thousand Miles

A Poet

A poet
likes to go
it alone sometimes.

A teacher,
part preacher,
mixing dogma with rhyme.

A prayer,
a line,
words, impeccable—so divine.

A kiss
before he goes.

Lost in time,
a million shows.

Upon Commencement

You leave an imprint,
no matter how small.
You see it in their eyes
when they greet you.

They ask if you'll take a photograph with them,
one that will end up in some graduation album
or on a dark, dusty shelf,
one they might pull out 5, 10, 20 years from now

and ask, "Who was that guy?"
You hope you left
an imprint somewhere.
Was it in their mind or their soul or both?

That was your aim,
to stretch them and yourself
to encourage their seeking
and thirst for knowledge.

Along the way
you prayed many times
the imprint would remind them
of their responsibility to themselves and to others.

It was the search that counted,
others that counted,
honesty with oneself that counted,
a search that never ends.

You remind yourself to love and forgive;
you did your best.
You smile for the snapshot next to your robed students,
hoping the imprint might last longer than the photograph.

Christmas Lights

She turns the Christmas lights on every year
after she puts
them in the window, on the tree,
and over the shrubs.

She lights the flame
in the luminaries
and stokes the
fire.

She ignites the oven,
creating dishes
we can only dream of
tasting and devouring.

Most of all,
she lights our hearts.
she lightens our souls
with her love and laughter.

She has created
the traditions
we now celebrate
as our own.

We know
from whence comes
The Christmas Spirit,
the joy of this blessed season.

In this and every season
her loving sacrifices
are examples
for us all.

She does light our hearts,
this woman we call
wife, mother, Mimi,
daughter, and friend.

We know
she understands
the true meaning
of Christmas,

And that is why
it is so appropriate
she lights
all the lights,

Today—
and every day.

The Game (a tribute to the Western Big Six)

I

Far away from the shrill of shrieking teens,
supersonic, screechy, fanatic screams,
cheering out loud for players and teams,
hoping the end will justify the means.

Far away from the stench of sweat-drenched uniforms,
unwashed socks and jocks,
Rawlings balls and Master locks,
from tear-away pants rarely torn, and athletes in vibrant
    jerseys adorned,

Far away from decent men in stripes,
gallant, upon their intent to assure fair play,
from pep bands and parents' gripes
blaring and blasting each in their own way,

Far away from the Rocks' press,
Blue Devils without a dress,
Panthers black and sleek,
Pioneers tenacious, rarely meek,

From Maroons in shades of purplish red,
and Streaks of gold and silver;
grateful all, scraped and bled,
hoping, in this season, a championship to deliver.

II

Far away from nights filled with buses' noxious fumes,
from cheerleaders' frightening flips and odorous perfumes,
from hot dogs gobbled down, so hastily consumed,
and ancient school songs sung innocuously out of tune.

Far away from the thrill of a battle fought—
a well-planned strategy,
preached, practiced, and patiently taught—
an unpredicted victory.

Far away from coaches and players,
connected in a sort of mystical way—
a basket, a steal, a magical play.
Wins and losses. Smiles, hugs, tears, even prayers.

III

Far away, there still remains
the memory of a game;
so pure, so chaste, so full of joy;
a ball, a basket, a little girl or boy.

As youngsters we, players past, dreamed of heralded fame,
Envisioning the legends we'd become.
Game after game, we'd light our inner flame,
march forth proclaiming we were number one.

We traveled gym to gym, from place to place—
each a sacred space,
steeped in glorious tradition.
Intent on winning, we discounted any possibility of loss,
surrender, or submission.

Those days, for us, are now gone by.
As players, charges drew,
and tossed balls through
rings of hardened steel and netted twine.

Sprinting across floors of inset wood—
emblazoned with a school's intricate center-court design—
final shots swished through rims of orange—as they should—
sealing victory—when games were squarely on the line.

IV

Memory transports us back
to moments—fleeting fame
where once we ran, passed, shot, attacked,
defending our goal, our school, our name.

Our reward was brazen celebration.
Passionate, fiery participation
on blustery, snowy, winter nights,
where we sought immortality under evening's brightest lights.

Some of us sit quietly now—gathering up our days of youth;
leaf through scrapbooks, which rarely tell the entire truth.
We hold tightly on to moments, recalling friend and foe,
the ones we've lost, brothers and sisters we'll always cherish so.

V

Such a simple tale, transcending space and time,
of our sport's soul mates then and now, replete with rhythm, a
    little bit of rhyme.
Much has changed, but much remains the same. Far away or near,
we love the game we hold so dear.

Hold tight, young lads and lasses, to your not-too-distant future,
where your games will soon be played,
where coaches teach and nurture,
and fans will have their say.

The ball will bounce, be passed, and tossed up ten-feet high.
Aspirations push you forward, rarely thinking of good-bye.
It comes to all. The game—gone too soon—the final buzzer makes
     it so.
Seasons gone by whisper with regret, "The clock's expired, now
     it's time to go."

VI

Far away memories sustain us—
entertain us,
affording us the luxury
of reliving moments long gone by.

All those games.
All those names.
All those places.
All those faces.

But the game,
ah, the game.
it will not be gone.
Not now, not ever

The game lives on.

Old Friends

"Time it was and what a time it was
A time of innocence
A time of confidences."

FROM "BOOKENDS" BY PAUL SIMON

We've won some games,
built buildings and refrigerators,
passed laws and defended a few, taught students, apprentices,
and Line workers.

No monuments or museums dedicated to us—yet.
A few newspaper articles
about how we won or lost or quit or caught a fish
or boosted some athletes.

We talk together about many things:
politics, sporting events, the economy, ethics, movies, parenting,
    and God.
Some of us are experts;
some of us merely claim to be.

We gather for special events:
weddings, funerals, commencements,
the Fourth and New Year's Eve,
when we quietly reflect upon endings and beginnings.

We're friends in the purest sense,
not expecting much,
not demanding much,
just being there when we can and when we're needed.

We've tried to be faithful to wives, children, churches,
    and communities.
We've not been perfect,
but we've mostly been honest with each other
and the others with whom we've associated.

We're not special, nor extraordinary.
We're men who sometimes go to our caves,
comforted by the reliability of a remote control,
asking only for some peace and quiet,

far from screaming crowds, constituencies, or labor leaders,
from pressures only we understand.
Deep inside we appreciate
each other and, perhaps,

that is why our friendships have endured
even across years and miles.
We look forward to being
with each other.

It's sort of like wearing our favorite comfortable slippers
or tattered flannel pajamas.
Such friendship
is authentic.

It consists of the people
you can rely upon.
The ones who make you laugh so hard you cry,
even during the toughest times.

We're not innocent anymore.
We understand the confidences required to be courageous.
We've given each other that when we most needed it,
in the midst of chaos or misunderstanding.

Nothing sentimental or schmaltzy,
nothing phony or corny,
We're always just there for each other when we're needed.
It's what friends do for each other.

Being there, in one way or another, at all times.
Such friendship defies description,
moves beyond the sorts of things we
understand and are able to explain.

Like so many other things,
we know it simply by its presence.

Poetry (merely a thought)

Why write it
or read it?
The poetry that is—

Matter of preference,
of living
over existence?

Matter of reflection,
of aberration
over frustration?

Matter of adoration,
for being here
to read, to write, to be?

Maybe.

Why not?

Creation of the Essence

If I had given you a mind for mathematics,
would you still have gone slow,
thoughts imploding and exploding
from mind to paper and back to thought?

Or would you have rushed to
find the answer lurking
in the formula or equation
closer to reason than to your soul?

If I had given you a mind for science,
would you still have
stared in wonder at the sunsets and the roses,
while questioning my existence?

Or would you have been
more immersed in the essence
of photosynthesis
while finding the cure for some obscure disease?

Not that solving problems
or curing disease is contrary.
Rather we must appreciate
what it is we possess.

You may bring life to metaphors,
connect the dots
and complete the picture,
even if the colors extend beyond the lines.

Your creation, much like mine,
may be intended to cause one
to pause somewhere along the path
and be grateful for what they've received.

Lessons Learned

They taught me to throw and catch,
balls and barnyard chickens;
taught me jump and hook shots,
and the splendor of written words and side-splitting jokes.

They taught me about devotion to family,
children,
country,
and a loving God.

They taught me to appreciate the joy of music,
sports, Swedish and Chinese cuisine, Coney hot dogs,
and other little things too numerous to mention.
They taught me the value of chores done well.

They taught me criticism
can be instructive and nonjudgmental.
Their praise was a gift
I perpetually sought.

They taught me to cherish each day
in loving honor and remembrance
of the loved ones
lost from the earthly grasp of our outstretched arms.

These lessons—not soon forgotten.
These lessons—guide me daily.
These lessons—taught with patience, kindness, and love,
by my aunts and uncles who remembered me, as I now
  remember them.

For like my parents,
they have loved me from the day I was born.
They loved me and taught me as if I was one of their own,
because I am.

At O'Hare

I carry the prayer with me
in my briefcase,
in my heart.
You and the prayer are both there.

Waiting for my flight,
I observed a man
being met by his children
and his wife.

He greeted them with a smile,
then kissed both of his children,
but not his wife.
I wept inside, aching and wondering,

what happens to marriages?
Where does the bloom of love go?
Do the storms crush us
or are we simply trampled by the years?

Do our gardens sit stark
perpetuated in browns and grays
nourished only by pain,
swept away by yearning?

I would have kissed you,
I would have held you,
I would have embraced all of you,
passionately anticipating our private moments.

I would have looked into your eyes
and you would have been assured
all of life, each moment
would bloom full.

That is our prayer—all of us
who feign mortality,
to be loved, cherished,
adored.

It is a prayer for ourselves
and for each other,
let us caress our existence
amidst the chaos.

Whether arriving or departing,
alone or with those we love,
we must find time
to acknowledge our beloved's presence.

Lean eagerly into the moment,
hold tight to the reunion,
dreading the thought of being separated
from our reciprocal gaze.

And when, at last, we retreat
lost in each other's arms,
we would rejoice at the discovery
of what had only been temporarily misplaced.

We would gently place
the prayer between our bodies,
calling upon our souls to store
it in a safe place guarded by our love.

As your eyes close to sleep,
I stare distantly into the twilight,
secure in our love
and reverently protect the prayer.

Assured it is the one sacred thing
we share with all of our being.
It connects us with meaning
and nourishes us to bloom full.

I watch you sleep,
kiss your gentle cheek,
close my eyes to dreams yet to be
where you and I become we,

where our departure always
signals the hope of still another arrival,
sealed with a kiss, secured with a prayer,
and the efflorescence of an eternal promise.

Papa's Song

Learn it all in intervals,
a bit at a time and never think
you ever have it all figured out.
Take each syllable and vowel,

and read all you can. You won't remember it all,
but you will remember most of what's important
to you, and let that sink in for a while,
let it become a part of who you are, but only a part.

Listen to what others say,
read their creeds or philosophies.
Make your own just that—your own.
Learn the formulas and understand the equations,

shapes and scientific method, all of those are important.
They will impact your world.
Formulate your own thoughts though.
Push equations to the edge of their respective paper rectangles.

Push yourself out of the box some.
Color outside the lines on occasion
because it's different and it's creative,
and it might help you better understand the world

when it moves somewhere beyond Pooh, Clifford, Bob the
    Builder, and Barney.
Above all, pay attention
to all of nature that surrounds you,
including people.

Learn about places, plants, how to make a good pizza,
and even write a poem once in a while.
Tell the world how you feel,
how thrilled you are when the leaves turn,

and how, when the snow has fallen, you can see back
into the deepest, darkest part of the forest in the winter
(where Bezel may live).
Don't be afraid to wonder

what mystery surrounds the flight of the geese
when they gather at the lake.
It all comes in intervals.
Take advantage of learning more about each mystery.

You won't ever know it all,
but you can know much about some.
Begin to understand
the mysteries you can, one by one.

Not all mysteries should be understood.
That is the greatest mystery of all.
I hope I beat you to that one.
In the meantime, I also plan on taking it all in,

one by one: observing your existence, your awe,
each new word, new discovery, new fact—
looking at the seasons
as they change and loving them all

for the unique mark they make upon our joyous souls
as we marvel at sunrises and sunsets.
I've learned a few things,
some important, some not.

What I do know came to me in intervals,
like each precious season.
Each in its own time, it settled in
and was a part of my existence.

You can't force it.
Just accept it, as a gift given.
Appreciate it and enjoy it,
each for its own beauty,

each for its own song,
sung in intervals,
sung in syncopation,
juxtaposed with the rhythm of life,

a rhythm that moves us forward each day,
forward toward some degree of goodness and mercy
found in each of our souls.
It's a movement performed in stages.

Learn to enjoy each mystery
for its own sake as you patiently watch it
unravel and gradually begin to accept
the truth as it is presented.

If you learn to accept the present
at each interval, then you will be given the greatest gift
     of all,
the acceptance of an all-knowing presence,
which only enhances your own presence, present,
     and prescience.

You'll have to figure that out
on your own,
in intervals each and every day.
Then you will sing your own song.

Herrick Lake in Winter

When you walk the trail,
regardless of the season,
it possesses idiosyncratic traits
that pays one little heed, especially in winter.

The fine gravel mix
caresses your feet,
unless ice remains
or the clay sits mud soaked.

The slippery slope
rises and falls
with each step,
whether certain or un-.

The sun beams down,
filtering through branches
and camps with the underbrush,
losing its flame in muted earthy colors.

If I gaze toward the course
or up to the heavenly clouds
or am distracted by a woodsy noise,
my stride might be broken.

My time is delayed,
my arrival postponed.
The bend that anxiously anticipated me
sits disappointed.

Eventually, I'll arrive
alone and move forward,
hoping to catch a glimpse
of what is patiently waiting.

The lake beckons,
frozen and white,
begging for the daring
to venture forth.

Geese gather
amidst garrulous calls
and decide upon a plan.
A leader sets the path.

They flap South
in seemingly effortless grace,
toward the warmth of their winter tomorrow,
pointed in the direction of survival.

Across the first bridge,
I surreptitiously glance west
toward the warmth of winter tomorrows,
toward the promise of all tomorrows,

around the north end
past the snow-capped grass,
where the picnics occur
prior to the canoe rides.

The return of the geese
marks a cause for celebratory exultation,
home at least for a while
until another season changes,

until all hell freezes over
and they are forced to decide
whether they will leave or stay,
die or survive.

Not my problem now,
legging the last lap of the journey,
headed toward the final bridge,
crossing over,

lost in flight,
swept into your arms
and the sweetness
of home.

Words

I've always been in love with words,
even when trying to make sense
of coaching a sport
or playing one.

I would try to find the words to describe
how it made me feel.
It was apparent that winning and losing were difficult
to describe to people who didn't really understand.

Sometimes the words come easy,
but more often they come hard,
pushed out in flinching labor,
difficult to rhyme.

Speaking metaphorically
is nearly impossible
when trying to describe one's life
to those who really don't understand.

It's not so much that they
don't understand; they just don't care
about my world, my joy, my sorrow.
They're, understandably, more concerned with their own.

Perhaps that's as it should be,
as we waffle in our narcissistic shells,
looking deeply and carefully into the mirror,
thrilled by the sound of our own words.

Whose words are they?
Do they belong to all of us,
or to just the few
who bother to listen, to care, to try to understand?

Regardless of all of that,
I still love words.

Paperboy

Climbing on my Schwinn,
with a canvas bag full of paper,
I trekked into the late-afternoon sun
or midwinter snow.

Throwing news to sundry porches,
to be read during evening's glow,
discussed over the dinner table,
then discarded, burned, tossed in the trash.

While collecting the weekly thirty-five cents required
for my labor—my daily diligence—
I witnessed real life
on Saturday mornings.

I rose early.
No cartoons in PJs.
Instead, I pedaled my route
to each home,

thanked the individual for answering the door,
and dropping the quarter and dime
into my other canvas coin bag,
earning a punch to their card. One down, thirty to go.

Real life—
sorrowful faces appeared, often unable to come up with
the thirty-five cents.

"Next week?"

"Okay, sure."

Real life—
naked toddlers sans diapers,
scurrying past,
visible through the crack in the door.

The stench
of filth and poverty
wafted through those doorway cracks—
stark, pungent boiled cabbage, soiled clothing.

Unfamiliar smells to me.
I remained oblivious,
always courteous and kind.
Boy Scout training, after all.

The daily routine found me tossing papers on porches—
Kubek to Skowron,
Starr to McGee,
Havens to Cannon to Sandburg.

Jeff, not Carl.
It was only later
I learned from one of my customers,
Mrs. Hinchliff,

about Carl,
her classmate, her friend,
a living legend in our little town and around the world!
He'd delivered papers, too.

Maybe throwing words around
is a prerequisite
for dreamers
and poets?

Then, again,
maybe it's searching
for life through the narrow cracks
in doorways.

Sweater Girl

It must have been sometime in December
nineteen sixty-eight,
after Dr. King and Senator Kennedy were shot
and killed.

Idealism ran rampant amongst us,
filled with rage and enthusiasm
for change
and also fear.

Where was our future?
Had we totally abandoned the greatest generation
with our sacrilege and profane disregard
for the nation they had created?

I imagine we seemed arrogant
in our assuredness of political rightness
as we waved our manifestos, held up symbolic finger(s),
and later begged, along with Lennon, to give peace a chance.

Have things changed that much?

We immerse ourselves in sundry nomenclature,
centering on the notion of social justice,
and cringe at the thought of internet predators
intent upon stealing away youthful innocence.

It remains a complex world
caught in a quagmire of oil—
digitized, energized, homogenized,
spiritualized, and compromised.

We gather though during the holiday season,
once called Christmas by most,
and bow in humble acceptance of
inclusion and pluralism,

in hopes such acquiescence
will somehow make this a less perilous planet.
It certainly holds us to some of those ideas
thought and spoken so long ago,

but I wonder as I wander,
"Do the church tower bells toll the end to this season?"
Have we sold our souls?
And for what good reason?

Have things changed that much?

* * *

Oh, yeah, back to December 1968.
It was somewhere in Macy's,
in New York,
Christmas shopping with my teammates.

I was thinking of you,
wanting to be with you,
remembering your eyes so blue,
your sweet smile—right on cue.

Snow fell soft on Herald Square,
floated down on Broadway between 34th and 35th
(Just like in *Valley of the Dolls*).
Frozen stiff, I walked into the 7th Street entrance.

I couldn't wait to get home to you,
bring you gifts, carefully chosen,
watch your face light up
and receive your warm embrace.

I roamed around
a bit bewildered, as usual,
up to the seventh floor,
then I saw it.

The mannequin posed—almost angelic,
arrayed in a white Angora sweater trimmed in navy blue.
My heart pounded in anticipation
of seeing it on you.

I think of such moments often,
of those days of innocence,
of butterflies dancing inside me
when I would be gone and then return.

Have things changed that much?

The gifts then were a mere token
of how I loved you,
how I appreciated you,
how much I missed you.

* * *

It's Christmas morning once again.
Once in a while there's a poem written;
always a gift given
meant to signify that same love and appreciation.

Our world has revolved and evolved,
but some things remain the same.
The dreams we held to so tightly are likewise—
some have changed; some remain unchanged.

In the final poetic analysis,
have things really changed that much?

I suppose.
We've both been witnesses to that.
But what, at least for me,
has remained the same?

I still believe in Christmas—
all it represents,
and I'm still madly in love
with you.

A New Day

She leaves behind the path marked yesterday,
tossing aside vines and shrubs that block the way.
A new path leads her toward a perfect light
as love breaks through darkened night.

The clearing sits green and bright.
She forges ahead, rejecting fright,
the path seems right,
the one marked Truth is now in sight.

Twigs she breaks;
splits fallen logs.
A fire she makes;
lies in warmth with faithful dogs.

Night again has come and gone—
with joyful heart she greets the dawn.

A Nurse and a Sailor (A song)

Upon the roof you got your start.
A love so enduring it would not stop.
You sailed apart,
your love did not.

Understood each other's pain
through every season, every rain.
Through births and deaths, you cried,
but a love like yours will never die.

Years pass so swiftly by;
heavenward you sent your sighs,
bittersweet prayers, as night goes nigh—
hello-goodbye, hello-good-bye.

Your love remains the same.
No regrets when He calls your name.
A love like yours will never end,
a love like yours will never end.

For sixty years your love's been strong;
in each other's arms—
where you'll always belong.

by Matthew and Barry Swanson

When Tulips Come to Our Backyard

When tulips come to our backyard,
gone is winter cruel and hard.
Icy-cold pauses, passes through,
gives way to spring, warm and new.

Blossoms ensure better days for all;
light prevails, insects buzz, grass stands tall.
Joy emerges, makes its way;
raised coffee cups—promise of another day.

Morning prayers—a lively chat or two.
Flowers and plants idly push through daybreak's dew.
Love blooms amidst such strife,
bound in bouquets of experience and life.

Spring delivers upon her sacred vow,
sending beauty here and now.
Promise and commitment remain as true
as you to me and me to you.

Swan Reflection

Eyes allure,
connections occur

in human fashion,
animal attraction.

Anxious lovers
drifting toward each other.

Emotions surge;
souls merge

in celebration,
in reflection

of what was,
what is,

and what is to be.

In reflection,
in celebration

of you
and all you mean to me.

The 2010s:
Every Teardrop
Is a Waterfall

Somewhere in New York

"Try to remember when life was so tender…"
"TRY TO REMEMBER" FROM *THE FANTASTICKS*
BY TOM JONES AND HARVEY SCHMIDT

When the silver aluminum train pulled out of the CB&Q station
and headed east to Chicago
we sat in separate seats,
pretending the other didn't really matter.

When the train pulled into musty Union Station,
I resisted looking at you,
flirted with the other girls
and pretended you didn't really matter.

We reloaded suitcases
into expansive baggage cars,
not unlike the confusing baggage we carried
from the awkward years of our youthful past.

We glided into Penn Station,
where the stench of the city by Madison Square Garden
wafted through grates,
then swirled aromatically around 31st Street.

We toured through Chinatown,
a disparate, unlikely couple
in red and orange,
but others saw it clearly.

As long lines delayed our passage to the wonders of the world,
Roger entertained the masses; we offered feeble accompaniment.
Lincoln seemed almost real,
I thought the same about you.

You seemed so out of reach,
but then something softened.
I nearly fainted.
Was it from the heat or a burning realization

that somehow you were the one,
and how could I ever have you?
Then there was the sweetness of your mother,
the photographic attention of your father.

As we sang with all our souls at the American Pavilion,
then sat together heading home,
it was as if I had remained in a sort of haze.
It all seemed surreal,

you, with your head on my shoulder,
and a lifetime ahead of us.

The Walking Stick

The trail is wrought with oak leaves in
clusters and fallen branches.
Others have tamped down clay
to make a tried-and-true path.

Melodies play in my ears,
stirring my soul,
lifting me up
to a higher place,

beyond mendacity,
beyond triviality,
beyond pettiness,
and jealousy,

Taking me back
to when I was young
and foolish.
Perhaps not much has changed in that regard.

A fallen branch
serves as a walking stick.
Although unwieldy,
it will do.

Once a branch arched
high over the trail,
brimming with life,
bright with green leaves

connected to the giant oak,
standing majestic,
smiling at the
saplings below.

Tiny pines unite with those saplings.
They stretch and emerge out of the soil,
learning the laws of the forest
in due time.

The lake lays still and blue.
Through barren branches
there's a prayer for other chances,
to feel renewed.

The moment's good.
Through tangled wood,
tomorrows wait,
ascend through a narrow gate.

The walking stick—
straight, anew,
steady, sturdy, never quick.
The sun sets, day is through.

We gather—
talk into night
about things that matter.
What is fair and just and right?

Here's a place
to now be free
to think, to sing, to write
maybe, just to be.

Metaphor and song struggle to explain
the mystery of the sun,
the falling of the rain.
Morning comes and we run

on old trails tried and true,
on trails untried, fresh and new.
With love we make our way,
grateful for the promise of today.

The Trail

When there is time
we can walk the trail
and arrive
at my favorite place.

A fallen log
sits nestled in the trees alone on a small hill
facing west
with a view of the lake.

There I often think about you
and your tomorrows
and the trails
you will walk.

* * *

This place affords a view
of a vista far below.
A song of tomorrows sung low
whispered soft and new.

Together we'll navigate the impeding gate,
me and my faithful mates,
descend from the hill above
home again and back to love.

There's a warm, brown house,
and behind a bright blue door
a love so true, Mimi, my spouse,
who we all adore.

We drink together our morning brew.
Cookies bake, a nap with Pooh,
forts are built and space stations too—
spaceship mix for a worthy crew.

Today the family celebrates,
as the trail sits still and waits.
We gather together here in great joy, time and space to say,
love to all on this dear and blessed Christmas Day.

A Partial Emergence

It tugs and pulls,
insisting it
be put down—
typed or scribbled

on yellow tablet,
a paper napkin,
the back of a small notecard,
already filled with a grocery list.

It won't let go,
pushing out of my brain,
down through sinewy hands
emerging half-formed,

making sense only to me;
to start,
being shaped to make
some sense,

to leave some message
of being,
to tell a partial story,
for all stories are, in fact, only partial.

Can't tell it all,
even if you want to,
but it insists.
I give it go,

hoping it will
make some sense.

Second Chances

At the Noshville Diner in Nashville
I sat with you as we ate;
you, oatmeal—me, eggs, sausage, and toast.
We'd filled up earlier on Amy, Vince, and the Predators.

You departed—temporarily.
I observed another booth.
Friends—one behind sunglasses
in bright running shoes,

the other a blonde
from a bottle.
She, the character,
joking, driving the conversation.

Both heads thrown back,
laughing—sheer joy,
the ecstasy of real friendship
over pancakes and eggs.

Joyfully starting over,
a new morning
emerging through the giggles
like, like, you know, like junior high girls.

A conversation
over who knows what,
but then does that
really matter anyway?

We had seen that two nights before;
 a couple taking full advantage of a second chance,
laughing, singing, being
joy-filled.

I'm grateful for all of mine,
and the love that accompanies
oatmeal, pancakes, eggs, etc.
at the Noshville Diner and beyond.

See Dig Run

Amongst the trees and budding limbs,
through the tall grasses and fallen branches,
down through narrow trails,
and wild shrubs and scattered leaves,

Dig, the deer runs free.

The forest is his sanctuary,
his holy place,
his cathedral,
his temple.

His existence is dependent
upon his ability to learn
and adapt,
to apply his knowledge.

He runs on instinct
with confidence
and self-assuredness,
embracing his freedom.

He is a creature of God,
carefree and innocent,
surrounded by the peace of the forest,
a peace *you* might seek,

There—

amongst the trees and budding limbs,
through the tall grasses and fallen branches,
down through narrow trails,
and wild shrubs and scattered leaves.

There—

in the peace of God's infinite nature,

There—

in God's peace that transcends all understanding.

Caution at the Crossing

The dark and weathered face
of the school crossing guard,
nestled in his stocking cap,
on a raw October afternoon

caught my eye
as I passed by,
in a hurry,
speeding along in a half-crazed flurry.

The bridge had long since disappeared
in my rearview mirror.
Home, oh so near.
The children stood frozen, no sense of fear.

The light signaled stop, don't go.
A lesson from long ago
emerged through my memory loss.
"Look both ways before you cross."

Important to recall the sage
crossing guard's warning at any age.
An adage true enough,
wise advice—good stuff.

What we were taught
lingers on in a single thought
with one, single caveat,
as we seek what should be sought.

Don't just look as you flee,
but rather, take the time to *see*
both sides, as you cross cautiously,
observing life's evolving mystery.

Pneuma

As November's final sun enveloped me,
I sat in the Adirondack chair facing southwest
with a book
and quiet,

(except for workmen's chatter down the cove
and the rustling of the leaves).
Traces of pneuma snuck up
in a restless breeze from behind.

The honeybees weren't bothered
nor was I.
The book talked of it,
in so many ways.

It sat with me, silent, and stayed for a while.
For a few moments, I paid attention to it,
gave it its due
even held it close.

Then in total and complete silence,
through my tears,
I tried my best to freeze the moment,
hoping I might always remember.

A Summer's Day in Steamboat, Colorado

There are glimpses
at dawn's earliest light, peeking through the haze
or gazing at the clouds
resting majestically—obscuring the life-giving rays.

There are glimpses
while in awe viewing the peaks topped off with ice and snow,
the multifarious flowers stretching across the steep hillside,
or tucked away in the green, lush forest.

There are glimpses
while wending along the street, negotiating with a fair-minded
    Shopkeeper
or being tended to by a server intent on actually serving.
All types of people, helpful and happy to be a part of life's
    intrinsic joys.

There are glimpses
while at play in the midst of a breathtaking botanical garden,
picnicking by a swift river,
or seeing the unabashed glee of old and young in pools and on
    slides.

There are glimpses
drenched in the natural waters falling into fish-filled creeks,
strawberry fields spawning mineral springs,
and a lake of pearl, so clear you can see its deepest secret.

There are glimpses
in physical specimens: bikers, hikers, hang gliders, runners,

a fit, elderly man (who told us his name was Henry) and his
    ageless wife,
all making the most of their moments.

There are glimpses
in the books we read, discuss, and argue about
as we process thought to print and then recycle
into our own sorted ideas.

There are glimpses
given ever so briefly of love and benevolence,
sheltering us from the mountain's storm,
protecting us from the lightning of unknowing.

There are glimpses even as we change our perspective,
moving from atop the mountain or up from the river,
to a place where we gaze inward then heavenward,
standing thankful for the glimpses we receive.

But we seek in the mist for more,
searching for a place
where we can truly soar
to humbly accept a loving Grace.

Perhaps,
it is there a glimpse turns into a vision,
as we realize we have only witnessed a mere portion,
of dwelling in the Presence while receiving a blessed assurance.

It is there we may discover the glimpse
was a brief, privileged preview
of our most fervent prayer,
to love and be loved with the utmost care.

Autumn's Dance

They dance, hurry, scurry,
sprinting, flying—an impetuous flurry,
hustling, bustling, rustling across the road
floating some, but never slowed.

Through barren field and lonesome lawn
racing forth in morning's dawn,
jumping, pushing in a rush,
detained too soon by hedge and brush,

to slowly rot and seep back down,
in loam and grass, the darkened ground.
Winter's grasp of autumn leaves
succumbs—staccato-like retreats and grieves,

yields to buds blooming up through snow
to flourish anew—to live and grow.

When the Blue Heron Touches the Moon

The blue heron soared overhead,
higher than normal.
The quarter-moon
hid in the plain sight of daylight beneath white clouds.

A Carolina blue sky framed spindly, dead limbs
endeavoring to reach heaven,
but it was too far away.
The limbs stretched upward, sinister, with no purpose.

The southern current pulled me north
toward indecision,
sinful in its own right,
attached to its own scarlet letter and all.

Then it dragged me back south,
filled with rejection,
a reaction to my antiquity.
But I am a poet.

Shouldn't that count for something?

If I morphed into even a half-moon,
where would I hide?
Along the forest path?
Inside the boathouse?

Trying to find myself,
searching for some sense in all of this,
by forgiving myself
and staying the course.

Currents sweep by.
Unknowing we succumb
to the temptation of the relevant moment,
seeking a cure, a solution—redemption.

Waiting for someone to really love us
as we were meant to be loved:
without condition or expectation,
understanding our insatiable needs.

Wouldn't that count for something?

How is it
I can be so easily attracted,
lured into places I don't even understand
or comprehend?

Pushed by currents
north and south
leading to some sort of
a nihilistic existence,

afloat in my own universe
oblivious—
to all of it,
to everything?

Wondering when I'll ever grow up.
Wondering if the limbs will ever reach heaven,
or if the heron will ever touch the moon,
or if my words will ever have real meaning,

and actually count for something.

Slipping Away

It slips away
and you don't even know that it is.
Beginning in your mind
the concept or the idea

is interrupted by
voices and various distractions,
worst of all a meeting.
And then you've lost it.

A notion that might change the world
or at least your world.
Words crafted so carefully—
gone.

Slipping away
slipping away,
no poem, no novel,
no song.

Slipping away.
Going, going, gone.

To the Boathouse or Ruminations Near the End of March

The screen door clatters closed.
Descent.
A broken door opens.
Sanctuary.

Replete with purported knowledge,
dust balls, ancient relics of triumph,
pictures of love, of great days,
and promises of serenity.

A little brown jug,
a nod to Glenn Miller and Grandpa.
A purple heart,
a nod to Philip, the soldier.

A ticket to the Exit Inn,
a meaningful hall pass,
a treasure—
me—imagine.

A golden ball,
a typewriter,
both ripe with stories.
Statuesque—silent.

A reliquary.
This boathouse of mine,
with a view
so holy, so divine

I pinch myself
in wonder
as I sit here
at this juncture

observing creation
an ever-evolving celebration,
thrilled with the notion of construction,
terrified by the threat of destruction.

Think, read,
write, share.
The process,
remember?

To create
is to live,
to be,
or choose otherwise.

Purported knowledge.
Who decides?
Where to?
What now?

Dirt piled high,
grass under straw,
the rule of law—
really?

By whose law do we abide?
In what century will we turn the tide
and find the key,
embracing love, forsaking misery?

The curlicue and period
end the thought,
but seeking answers
remains our lot.

Retreat, regroup,
abandon liars, lies,
Revise, revise.
Just tell the truth.

At least your own,
the best you can.
Seeds shall be sown,
pray creation will withstand.

An Acrostic from Papa

Read all you can.
Imagine all you can.
Grow all you can.
Help all you can.
Think all you can.

Write all you can.
Achieve all you can.
Yearn for all you can.
Share all you can.

When You're Smiling

"Who can turn the world on with her smile?"

FROM "LOVE IS ALL AROUND"
MARY TYLER MOORE SHOW THEME SONG
LYRICS BY SONNY CURTIS

Where do we begin?
The two of you?
BFF?
And you let me in.

On a hard hallway bench
you counseled,
cajoled, laughed,
even coached a bit.

You stood or sat by her side
at Pioneer games, Lake Bracken movies,
a summer in Bloomington, a July engagement,
a January wedding,

even tougher times,
when men get stupid
or an insidious disease disrupts everything
or when life as we know it goes awry.

You were there, with your smile.

Even miles away,
on the phone,
with a text,
or a surprise visit.

At a lake in Iowa
(who even knew there was
such a thing?)
we gathered.

We were family,
at least it felt so.
Jammed into a cabin
that strangely felt like home.

We swam, read, sailed, floated,
some of us dove.
A treasure trove
of memories.

And you were there, with your smile.

We also wept
at glorious births,
enchanting weddings,
and devastating deaths.

We discovered
our strengths and weaknesses.
Ideas came and went,
as did occupations and relationships.

We have all evolved,
and planted our seeds
for tomorrow,
but we still stand by each other.

That's what love does—
it transcends everything.
it brings meaning
to celebration.

That's what we feel
deep in our souls
for you, on this special occasion,
on your day.

And now, we are here, all together,
so happy, once again, just to see your smile.

The Early 2020s:
Run to That Future

Pollen

The pollen covers most everything at the lake
this time of year.
It doesn't discriminate,
just blankets

chairs, tables, sidewalks,
umbrellas, boat covers,
Solo stainless-steel fire pits,
and my car.

That's the least of our worries
now.
Would prayer help?
What about listening to the medical experts?

Doesn't do much good to whine.
I suppose many folks feel
unappreciated,
especially doctors and nurses.

I take a deep breath,
soak up the sunshine,
watch the flow of the lake's current,
and listen to the buzz of the carpenter bees

as they eat away at our home.
They seem innocuous;
so did the coronavirus.
What if we had listened?

At the Galway Hooker

The fiddler plays,
Irish dancers stomp away.
Guinness flows—Tullamore Dew,
Jameson, too.

Shots we snatch,
down the hatch,
quite a sight,
sweetness in morning's light.

Amidst the din,
a friendship that'll never end.
Irish egg rolls, Shepherd's pie,
Reuben sandwiches—corned beef stacked, two feet high.

Santa, St. Pat or Nick,
it matters not,
iPhone cameras click;
the fiddler plays "Come On Eileen" for the motley, drunken lot.

From the Hooker we, at long last, trot,
Arm in arm, a bit besot.
Memories tucked away in time,
friends together, like rhythm and rhyme,

we depart amidst afternoon's faded light.
Faded? Never a quiver,
not us, not ever!
Everything's gonna be alright.

Reunion

We wended our way
along disparate, egalitarian, Unitarian,
(but certainly not puritan) paths.

Up, down, about, and through
not our way, but thy way
was done.

To whom, from whom
arriving here and now
living—fully.

And glad to be doing so.

Night Sweeper

Train whistles cut through evening's light.
Doors close, street and porch lights gesture night.
Songs echo longingly through screens,
marking signs of other places, other scenes.

Thoughts—dormant, disregard rhyme
or reason—warning signs
of things to come;
elections lost and won.

Opinions fade into darkened night.
Cylinders whine, whistles fade,
charismatic promises made,
then disappear—ignominious—out of sight.

The Night Sweeper enters the street.
Sidles up to each and every gutter,
sweeps away debris and litter—
dawn breaks, mission complete.

What if we could do the same with lies?
Sweep them away,
expose them in the light of day.
Who might be so wise

to simply tell the Truth?

A Later, More Mature Version of a Previous Poetic Effort

I fashioned myself after none of them—the poets of old.
And, yet, in so many ways, many of them still influence me.
I've tried my best to uncover the world the poets seek,
    according to Emily in *Our Town*.

There exists, instead, the perpetual journey of mystery.
Fortunately, I've actually experienced very little misery.
Circumstances change, day by day,
make your bed, go your own way.

There's nothing particularly constructive about
seeking answers to eternal and confounding questions.
Embrace the physical universe,
let the rest just ride.

I doubt I could ever do that completely because I'm
    tragically involved
in a love affair, one that consumes me—
me and my words. We've tangled for so long.
I embrace some of them, even when I know they're
    all wrong.

Too possessive!
The same is true with feelings;
preoccupation with my existence.
I drop the pen, and try my best to abandon self-indulgence,
    self-aggrandizement,

intent on taking the time to think of others,
die to self, shed the confining shackles of narcissism,
celebrate life, and abandon all sense of mourning.
Did any of those ancient poets ever say that?

I bet they did—
in one way or another.

A Sibling's Love

What is this feeling
wrought so deep in
my thoracic cavity?
Is that my soul

crying out
to be heard,
to be recognized,
to be accepted

for who
I really am?
Who, I believe, you know me
to be.

You wrote
me a note
many years
ago.

You wrote
of your faith,
your deep abiding
faith.

You live
that, it seems
to me,
every day.

Your loving care
for your husband,
your children,
your grandchildren.

You picked up
where Mom
left off—
unconditional love.

Cards,
phone calls,
long drives
back home

to honor

them;
they who
taught us
so much.

I believe
that feeling
I get deep inside
is due, in part

to what they taught us,
and gave so unselfishly
to us
from the first moment

they held us
in their arms,
kissed our foreheads,
and cared for us

until their last breath—

Love!

Your patience,
your kindness,
are a reflection
of that upbringing.

I admire
you for so many reasons
but I never
tell you that.

I sit
in gratitude
for you,
blood of my blood.

You have known me
for the longest.
You who know
my strengths and weaknesses.

Let me write two
things
which might
express it best.

Thank you
for being you,
and for
loving me.

Just as
I love you.

Bountiful Earth

As you travel far,
may this bountiful earth sustain
who you are deep within.

Air

Like the air we breathe,
words arouse our very being,
spurring love into action.

Resilience

Flourishing flower,
lovely, cloaked in resilience
unremitting—strong.

Sunrise

Music stirs your soul,
lifts you beyond the mundane,
just like a sunrise.

The Planet's Wonders

Seek the unknown,
uncover the planet's wonders,
wisdom unearths humility.

Games

Games of youth preview
what we see in nature—
triumph and defeat.

Facts

Rhythm of life—undeniable.
facts—honest, honorable;
open heart and mind abide.

Oak Tree

Sturdy, strong oak tree.
Reliant in all seasons.
Perpetual protector.

Dancing Girl

Dance with utter joy;
leap, twirl, and spin—life's beats begin
as new seasons unfold.

Breeze

Vibrant, buoyant breeze,
rhythmically rustling through trees.
Nature's own music.

Beyond All Measure

Beyond all measure,
the elegant, protective pen
defends her cygnets.

Swollen Stream

Anxious swollen stream
Snow and Ice drift far apart
Salmon fight to spawn.

by Tim Granet

The Italian Village

We sat there,
as the seventh decade of the twentieth century stretched before us,
sharing Chateaubriand at the Italian Village restaurant.
Not very Italian.

So many things have changed since then.
They don't even serve
Chateaubriand at the Italian Village
anymore.

The meal was heavenly.
Hair was unique,
not your common
Broadway musical.

Such excitement
surrounded our lives.
The Carpenters later sang
"We've Only Just Begun," and we had.

There was no crystal ball
through which we could envision
our beautiful children, our lovely homes,
cancer, the death of our parents.

Vietnam was a *Nightly News* headline,
Kent State an unknown school in Ohio.
Kaiserslautern was not referenced in our German book.
The first of our great adventures.

And so it was,
and is still—a great adventure.

The Italian Village menu is framed
on our bedroom wall,
a reminder of a time we shared
Chateaubriand.

We've also shared our lives
with each other.
As Carly Simon sang,
"That's the Way I've Always Heard It Should Be."

Our honeymoon ended
less than perfectly,
but like all our adventures
it made a great story.

In the opening number of *Hair*,
the chorus sings, "Aquarius."
Somehow, I now I find those words
prophetic.

They seem to encapsulate
these many years
we've shared,
for the most part, "so happy together."

The long-haired, semi-nude Hippies belted it out,
singing about harmony, understanding,
sympathy, trust, ridding ourselves of falsehoods and derisions
and living with visions of golden living.

So, here's to the Italian Village,
Chateaubriand,
golden living,
and dreams of visions beyond our imagination.

Here's to us!

The Road We Take

I've traveled many roads—wending,
uncertain when the last will be ending.
Or, as dogwoods in spring—
just beginning.

Destinations, decisions,
ruminations, revisions.
Narcissism, stoicism,
dejection, rejection.

Stood at many crossroads considering
which way to turn;
contemplating
whether I might possibly earn

long-yearned-for hometown respect.
Was there an ancient self-inflicted curse,
only making worse
what I might hope for, or expect?

There was a desperate need,
beyond introspection, ceremony, or creed
one considered a holy treasure—
to be loved forever and beyond measure.

Searching afar,
in places common and bizarre—
from Jerusalem to Sydney,
aching to be free

of everyday monotony,
devious monopoly,
and callous indiscretion—
I prayed ceaselessly for redemption.

Avarice, a temptress, did her best to envelope me instead,
promising paths strewn with prominence that led
me toward my own quasi destruction.
When grace finally came, it offered a certain sort of
    resurrection.

Time to look where I'd been,
without regard for loss or win.
To exist, reflect upon the Good,
walk and think upon what I should.

Where had I been?
What roads home to and fro
had I traveled, where did I go?
What good had I done, where did I sin?

My roads were sundry—

    Park Lane Avenue
    Beecher Street
    Kellogg Street
    Jefferson Street
    Belle View Court
    East Street

Franklin Avenue

Kelsey Street

Sickenger Strasse

Rodenbach Village

North Street

Academy Street

Prairie Street

Stonegate Avenue

Fairview Road

Park Lane Road

Clark Cove Road

Around this sphere
we all call home,
I have, for years, aimlessly roamed—
traveling far and near.

A road here and there
proffered sanctuary
or sanctity, but where, oh, where
was there the slightest degree of sanity?

I chose
the roads I took;
some foreign, others close,
some through great cities, a few by stony brook,

made decisions at every fork;
some made sense, some did not.
Sacred some, others I forsook—
A risk is what I sought—this is what I got:

a life scattered—a small bit of regret,
yet, actually, far more joy.
Bliss is what some might call it.
The grateful life of a common boy from Illinois.

Where will my last road come to an end?
Is there an even greater road—just around the bend?
Not for me to know or say—a rolling of the dice,
But if it leads to a finer place, now wouldn't that be nice?

In Memoriam

Acciaccatura

Leaves fall gently.
You glance over the shoulder,
looking back,
you remember—

yesterday is gone.

Silently, wishing for flowers,
waiting for their arrival,
reveling at their appearance,
rejoicing in their being.

Today is.

Gently breezes sweep
leaves away. Yesterday departs.
Flowers exist. (They always do following winter.)
Dreams are made of things such as these.

Tomorrow.

for Susan Aldrich

In Memoriam

Centenary Celebration

They're throwing a celebration for you,
lots of folks who know lots of things.
Your daughters are here;
everyone is paying homage.

Howard K. and Gwendolyn B.,
amongst the talent making it a special gig.
You'd probably view it with a sense of humor,
all these notables making a fuss, calling you famous.

When I was a kid, they called you a worthless bum,
a political activist, a socialist, God forbid!
The erudite claimed your language was too simple.
Now it's full of the strength of the people of the prairieland.

You told the truth, my fellow Swede,
hard as that is for some to swallow.
With your pen, you mowed hypocrites down,
a few remain, pompous, still powerful, in our prairie town.

I regret never seeing you in person,
but I recall the Penny Parade—
your raucous rendition of John Johnson
squawked over the school's P.A.

I delivered the Galesburg Register-Mail newspaper
to an old friend of yours.
She would laugh and reminisce
about how you would come to town,

full of spirits—not, in the least, profound.
She'd pick you up at the station
treat you to some coffee
and drop you off at your room at the Hotel Custer.

Some memories make ordinary men great.
but you were far from ordinary.
Compassionate. A man of the people—Yes!
A visionary, a truth-teller.

Your 100th birthday was no disgrace.
As I sat awed in Otto Harbach's place,
listening to the learned. As your daughters spoke
about you and your beginnings, I awoke

to the greatness in you and your belief
in the common man, his ability to rise
from the muck, from tiresome grief,
to grasp his own integrity and pride.

Dignity is what some call it.
You gave credence to the fact that every man
should be afforded that right.
a universal manifest destiny was your plan.

Along the way you discovered those
whose prejudice and hatred were difficult to expose.
Hiding behind governments and boards,
the privileged made decisions (still do) where human decency's
    ignored.

Through struggle and unceasing nonsense,
you wrote to uncover the essence
of being aware
regardless of who or where.

Two lovers sat in front of me holding hands—evolved,
enraptured by your story, totally enthralled.
A moment captured in each other's warm embrace,
adoring it all, unabashed in such a public place.

The past, a wink, I thought.
O. T. Johnson's department store and lutefisk barrels are closed
    now.
Battles won and lost—bravely fought.
Always the young strangers—your final boast.

Here existed your illumination.
Before me the learned discussed your creation.
Enlightened to a degree, I realized how fortunate to be
in the unpredictable throes of humanity.

You were there once upon a time
making the most of your existence,
so remarkable, so sublime,
leaving us with an ongoing lesson in persistence.

A reminder to the entire world—
broad, sprawling, eager to embrace—to make a fuss,
to go forth ideals unfurled,
embracing your spirit in each of us.

As for the celebration,
it continues and continues and continues . . .

for Carl Sandburg

The Passing of a Young Child

From here to there,
we arrive and flee,
discovering what was,
what is, what's going to be.

Not knowing,
we fear
His awful grace
has unwittingly erased

this precious being.

Rain falls,
uncertain rhythm
ground to earth,
and beyond.

With the drops,
we go there, too,
in desperate search
of what to do.

This final place
where a child lies,
dressed in lace,
amidst our cries.

Why now, a soul so innocent, so free?
So much of life yet to see.
We stand, do our best not to fall,
sobbing, dying inside—a wailing wall.

From here to there,
we arrive and flee,
praying to rediscover
what life might once more be.

for Elise Bowen, Brandon Coffman, and Annah Fox

Edna's Flower

How is it at my age
I remember her
so clearly,
so distinctly?

The smell of the house,
especially the kitchen,
the watercolors and oils
that adorned the walls,

the rugs,
the buttons,
and the flowers. . .
always the flowers.

I recall them,
big and pink,
rosy-looking,
like her cheeks.

Her manner was as gentle
as her hands.
Her voice soft and mellow—
a classical recording.

She loved beauty—
in paint,
in poetry,
in crafts.

Her finest craft
was making
all of us
feel special.

She did pamper
us somewhat,
but that was
just her love.

It was that love
of which I was reminded
when I saw the flower—
Edna's flower—

an image,
etched in my mind,
carried through time,
her love came to me.

Sent through you,
it will endure through the ages.
A flower-like bloom
that will never fade.

The flower—a gift
from God.
Given in spring
again and again.

One of the lessons
she taught me
remains over all,
"Our Redeemer Liveth."

An ethereal memory
is much the same,
whether prompted by
photograph or senses.

So it was
when I saw
Edna's flower.
So it is now.

True enough;
our Redeemer liveth;
And in the depths of my soul,
so does my grandmother.

for Edna Ottoson and Betty Swanson

Coach

Oh, man!
It appears you're just a man, after all,
not a god,
like I once thought.

What really made you, you?
Very few had your fire.
Charismatic.
Enigmatic.

Once you confided in me,
told me about your mother,
who you adored,
but there were issues.

You became an athlete,
an extraordinary one,
multiple sports
a professional,

Bob Pettit, the St. Louis Hawks,
House of David;
hence,
the Pro philosophy.

Shoes, vitamins
(what was in those?),
charter busses,
rib eye steaks at Wong's—post game.

Style and class.
Uniforms—an embroidered silver lightning bolt
on the front and our name on the back.
An overhead scoreboard with our names hanging
    high above a packed gym.

We soared
to unexpected heights,
Then, an unexpected
mid-December stumble.

You regrouped us,
motivated us,
never losing faith
in what, together, we might accomplish.

You may have been a mere mortal,
but we believed in you, too.
We soared again, to the very end,
then stumbled one last time.

Memories of that season
remain intact.
The team,
you.

Oh, you were human,
yes, just a man,
not a god,
but you made us special.

I stand beside you,
here in your final resting place
remembering what you said
to me once, long after my playing days.

You said you loved us.
The feeling's mutual.
You led us to places
beyond our wildest dreams.

My prayer is you
are now forever
in such a special place,
one of everlasting peace and love.

for John Thiel

Prairie Son

"O prairie mother, I am one of your boys.
I have loved the prairie as a man with a
heart shot full of pain over love.
Here I know I will hanker after nothing
so much as one more sunrise or
a sky moon of fire doubled to a river of water."

FROM "PRAIRIE" BY CARL SANDBURG

O Prairie Son—

You knew of cycles, how life worked,
how to turn black prairie soil to green plants,
how to fatten the pig and calf,
even how to butcher them.

O Prairie Husband—

You knew how to make a wife feel special,
how to make her laugh and how to comfort her sorrow,
how to provide for her,
how to grow old together gracefully and with love.

O Prairie Father—

You knew how to make a daughter and her children feel loved,
how to teach them about the land you also loved,
how to survive in a world you often didn't understand,
and how to love each other as a family.

O Prairie Brother—

You knew how to make us all feel at ease and comfortable,
how to laugh with each other from brother-in-law to niece and
    nephew,
how to farm, how to bid at an auction, how to shoot, how to drive
    a tractor,
how to care about each other.

O Prairie Friend—

You knew of our woes and sorrows, of our good years and bad,
you were there in the coffee shops or the fields
with a good joke, a quick smile,
an understanding bit of advice.

And now, O Prairie Son—

You shoot pain in our hearts,
for we will miss you.
but you move on to another harvest,
and you will surely reap what you sowed.

O Loved One of the Prairie—

You knew of life's cycles.
Now you know all.
The last chore is done,
the livestock and the chickens are secure,

And so are we—

in the knowledge
you will rise in the morning with the Master
and begin a new day, as will we.
For the cycle you knew so well continues.

for Emery Conrad

Music Man

When pianissimos fade, too soft to be heard,
when crescendos crash so, I wish I were deaf,
when the treble becomes bass clef,
when melodies turn bereft, beyond absurd,

you'll still be our Music Man.

When all sopranos hit high C on key,
when all altos quit flittering incessantly
with tenors trying to be
as cool as the mellow basses, who pull it off effortlessly,

you'll still be our Music Man.

Music Man—

You gave us a happy hour plus so much more,
teaching us patience, kindness, and appreciation,
helping us to better understand ourselves. You opened the door
so we could truly experience music and its universal fascination.

When all the Broadway shows have closed,
when the Alps mountaintops are no longer frozen,
when thirteen eggs become a dozen,
when our faded memories of *The Fantasticks* have reposed,

you'll still be our Music Man.

for Roland Hegg

Battle Hymn

I hope it's not too late
to tell you how I feel.
I fear there are times
when you sit and stare,

residing in a place and time distant from us.
The gift you gave
to so many may now, simply,
be trapped inside your mind.

The smile remains whenever we
walk into the room, or when you "tickle the ivories."
We love those moments now, just as we loved them then.
Your smile was a sign of our collective success—yours and ours.

* * *

With my own smile,
I remember the first time
we officially met as a student and teacher.
It was an audition

held in a soundproof cubicle,
walled from floor to ceiling with acoustical tile.
How assuring it was to know
that if I fumbled a note on the scale

no one would hear it but you and me.
Your smile lit up that small room.
I felt comfortable almost immediately,
even though my voice box seemed

to be wrapped in a tight knot around my larynx.
(Is that the same thing?).
You kindly asked
me to sing some scales,

repeating what you played on the piano.
You struck the keys with confidence, rhythm, style.
I made it through the medium notes
but struggled with the high ones.

I soon discovered the notes
were a foundation for the songs
we would sing. Notes combined
with words to give meaning,

But that meaning paled in comparison to the relationships formed
in the room next to the cafeteria.
The music connected us to one another.
You connected us to one another.

It was a magical time in our lives.
We just didn't know how magical it was.
We were swept away by the gifts given to us
by the composers and you.

Even tough athletes began to understand
what it was like to feel emotions.
You were never very good at hiding yours.
The tears in your eyes were a dead giveaway.

The music touched all of us.

Through your example, you taught us
to feel the beauty and power
of a given moment through music.
That was not only a gift, but a lifelong wonder.

We were fortunate to experience
so many of those moments with you.
I suspect you felt the same way
about us.

We sang our last song together
on graduation night.
Our hearts were mixed with feelings
of sorrow and joy, our eyes full of tears

as we completed the final verse of
"The Battle Hymn of the Republic."
It was as if we were praising the whole wonderful experience
we had shared together.

"Glory, glory, hallelujah!"

That night concluded
a time in our lives
we will never forget,
etched forever in our minds.

We sat in our neat rows
of altos, sopranos, basses, and tenors
as you daily presented us the wonderful opportunity
to learn and appreciate music, but there was more.

It was the understanding
truth does march on
in our hearts and in our minds.
You imbued us with this sense

of respect and decency that went beyond
our knowledge of the music.
We were given moments of love, friendship,
and a greater appreciation

of what the music meant
to each one of us in our own lives.
It is that sense
I carry with me today

even as a middle-aged man.
It is a finer understanding
of what Kierkegaard
referred to as "the relatedness of a given moment."

I reflect often upon those days,
sitting in my leather-upholstered cubicle
(it's not soundproofed),
cranking up the speakers.

As the music reverberates through my soul,
I feel my lips quiver—
I become one with the music.
My eyes tear up as I am,

once again, moved by the music.
I whisper a prayer of thanks
for you and the gift
you gave us.

When I look into your eyes now,
I'm not certain how much
of what I say is understood.
But I hope you can understand

how grateful I am
you were a part of my life.
You taught me the truth about music,
you were and still are my friend.

I love you now, just as I loved you then.

You fight your own battle now,
just as we all do, looking for meaning.
What was it we sang amidst the beating of drums,
the clanging of cymbals?

It's all so appropriate now,
the final refrain of our last song.
It seems like only yesterday,
yet, it's like a song sung in another lifetime.

The refrain continues to ring loud and clear.
You remember—
"Glory, glory hallelujah, Glory, glory hallelujah,
Glory, glory hallelujah, His truth is marching on."

for Roland Hegg

Grandpa's Watch

Perhaps, I was somewhat like Grandpa's watch
lost, hidden in a box,
and no one knew where to find me,
not even myself.

Battered by years of abuse
by my own hands and the hands of others,
my inner workings had rusted,
and my sense of time was no longer accurate.

It seemed that no one wanted to conduct the search.
I was left to do it on my own,
seek answers everywhere,
as the hands spun helplessly, losing track of propriety.

I lay inert in the box.
It was comfortable enough,
secure and proper,
but I remained lost.

I sought your help,
but feared your raw honesty,
afraid of coming clean
and releasing the demons.

When I did,
it was similar to the mythical box.
The demons invaded our souls,
ripping open our hearts.

All time stood still,
watching and wondering
if we could survive
such chaos.

Tumultuously, we probed
our emotions,
trying to be as truthful
as humanly possible.

But a sacred trust
had been broken,
and the hands of time
spun out of control.

What was real now?
What was honest?
Who were we?
What were we to become?

In the secrecy and deceit
of our hearts,
we searched for the truth,
which was waiting to be found.

The realization was
we had to find ourselves first,
grapple with our own sins
and beg forgiveness.

In the depths of my dark box
a moment of serendipity came,
just like when I opened the box,
which had protected my grandfather's watch.

I realized that I'd been given the gift of choice,
free to maximize
my present
or wallow in my past.

He had opened the box many times
for me.
Sometimes I'd paid attention,
often, I'd ignored His grace,

wrapped in selfishness and humanness,
embracing my own pity,
locked into an empty existence.
I'd been enslaved by my pride.

So, when I opened
the box
and found Grandpa's watch,
I fell to my knees

in grateful appreciation
for His love
and
His forgiveness.

The watch is found,
I pray grace abounds.

Searching on,
I seek love and peace,
working my way out of the box,
in order to once again commence.

I want with all of my heart
to understand you,
to give to you,
to love you as if it was the first time.

With full knowledge that the hands are moving,
I proceed cognizant
time is precious,
and inevitably the box will close.

Then,
we may be given the privilege to fully realize
the transitional nature
of our experiences.

The treasures life contains
do not belong to us,
we hold them temporarily
extended by memory, then lost to eternity.

Such treasures must be passed
from generation to generation,
held in respect and high regard,
cherished and given in complete love.

Such an understanding
of love and abundance,
may enhance what we have shared.
This particular time we dared

to attempt to discover the truth
in our souls,
to be reborn
to the joy of living,

to love each other
the way we deserve,
to leave the legacy
that is our destiny.

We are bequeathing our honesty
by allowing the light
back into our lives,
and ordinary times.

Time passes.
Age withers us all,
but if we allow love to stay,
we'll not fall

away from each other's arms,
but into His.
Then we'll know
to fully embrace the moment

when we run once again
to join souls,
and understand what this
has all meant.

Until that eternal climb,
the watch that has at last been found
will chime, "Love now, love now,
It is time!"

for Ralph Ottoson

A Death Too Soon

Grandpa died too soon.
He didn't get the crops in that fall.
The job was left undone.
Grandma and the boys were left to fend for themselves.

I never got to sit in his lap,
feel his strong hands,
hear his Swedish stories or accent,
or even smell the pungent manure laced obscurely in the cracks
    of his boots.

He was conspicuous by his absence—
at all of my graduation ceremonies,
the State championship game,
our wedding.
He never held his grandchildren or his great grandchildren,
    not one of them.

His departure left a family in a state of grief and bewilderment.
Death was too real. It left too much of a void.
It was always too painful to mention, much less discuss.
We still dance around it.

I know God must think me selfish.
His plan is omniscient.
I can't match that. All I know for sure is
Grandpa died too soon.

for Fritz and Helen Swanson

The Hands of a Giant

Your greeting began with the "finger shake"
(reserved for a special few to make).
Thick digits—thumb and index finger.
squeezing lightly, never lingered.

The grizzly bear hug followed, as did your deep chuckle
rising from the depths of your massive torso
up from your bulging belt buckle,
supported by stitched knees and ankles bowed below.

Your hands—immense,
relaxed, hanging, rarely tense.
Hands—that sculpted a plate with the expertise of a gourmet chef.
Hands—that caressed a new born babe, even when bereft.

Hands—that would hoist a massive appliance,
or tame a stubborn remote into compliance.
Hands—that clapped encouragement for all,
rarely criticizing any, whether big or small.

Hands—that engulfed a small, white ball,
teed it up, smashed it far; from left to right it would pass,
a banana slice, you'd call. Miraculously, it would fall
occasionally, upon short, pastoral, fairway grass.

Hands—that crushed tension from a back or neck,
melting one into total submission,
like the wrestling holds you'd explain and correct,
patiently teaching with a rare sense of understanding and vision.

Hands—that would point us to a remote place,
a destination unknown by "Alice," the navigation box,
perhaps known only to one sly as a giggling fox,
reserved for pals—a special time and space.

Off we'd go—obscure diners or bars,
laughing out loud, hanging with the "common" man,
discussing sports, western movies, or cars.
You were just a simple guy, a buddy, a fan.

You knew no strangers, only friends—
old and new.
They gathered at the end,
especially the boys of summer, your traveling crew.

* * *

Our loss is now heaven's gain
as the Master's gentle hands
lead you, a good and decent man,
home to His eternal hall of fame.

Peaceful now in a holy place,
full of forgiveness and total loving grace,
embraced by Hands so immense
that hold you now and forever hence.

Your life was a model of congeniality
full of joy, humor, loyalty, and frivolity.
Your gentle eyes and winsome smile,
reminded us of the love you shared with us mile after mile.

You were a giant amongst us in oh, so many ways.
Memories sustain me now throughout the nights and days.
As I bid you a fond farewell and though my sorrow does remain,
I pray we will someday meet again in His eternal hall of fame.

for Steve Coffman

Empty Tables, Empty Chairs

"There's a grief that can't be spoken
There's a pain goes on and on....
From the table in the corner
They could see a world reborn
And they rose with voices ringing
I can hear them now."

FROM "EMPTY CHAIRS AT EMPTY TABLES" BY CLAUDE-
MICHEL SCHONBERG AND ALAN BOUBLIL, *LES MISÉRABLES*

The table and chairs now sit empty.
We dispersed
to the rain-soaked parking lot
and headed home.

Memories and stories
slid comfortably across the table,
back to the fall of 1966: lowly pledges,
Gulick Hall, Tobin's Pizza, phones at the end of a hallway

or ones you paid
so you could talk to home,
to someone you loved,
someone who remembered you

for who you were
and encouraged you
to become
even more.

We sat in small rooms,
beds facing each other,
Playboy Playmates pinned on cork,
vinyl records slid down spindles on to turntables; needles
    scratching out tunes.

Conversations were innocent then,
politics, sports, women.
We remained naive,
content to pull on a rope.

We evolved.
We were reminded by the band, Crosby, Stills, Nash & Young
that most of our changes would be there,
in a rusty, brown house on East Street,

where we gathered
at round tables,
listening to our Magister
instruct us in the ways of the cross.

We attacked Redbirds,
threw their bricks back at them,
shined shoes, polished floors,
made wake-up calls and stood in line-ups,

not realizing
we were being schooled
to live an exemplary life
of friendship and, yes, even love.

We lit the match,
Runkle, Bell, Lockwood, Jordan

Cooper, Scobey, Caldwell.
Fizz, Fuzz, Fizz-Fuzz . . .

The quest began.
What have we found?
The century turned
and phones got smart.

Cameras send
photos to Blogs,
and electronic mail
reminds us of who we were and are.

* * *

We gathered,
there at Lucca's,
there at the table
to remember Bois,

Bois—a magnificent mind, impish smile and chuckle,
an original in so many ways; sometimes arrogant, more often kind.
Spinning a phrase to astound or rankle.
Lecturing irreverently to shock or dazzle our simple minds.

There we sat firmly in our collective memory,
devouring Baldini pizzas, listening to Dunc's long-distance
     sorrow
through the chips in one of those smartphones,
sharing tales of days gone by, some true, some hyperbolic.

Faded photos, in dissipated color, black and white.
Laughter and tears, the night grew late.

Mac shared his tribute,
heartfelt and honest, just like Pat—first rate.

* * *

Around those dining room tables
inside that house on East Street,
we were taught the three great aims:
friendship, justice, and learning.

If ever one of our brothers
epitomized those words,
it was James Burnett Boisclair.
Gone from us too soon.

He fought the good fight.
His work now complete.
A life well lived, replete.
Luster to the cross—another aim for each of us.

"Spirits can never be divided that love and live in friendship."
Reciprocal is the bond we share
in this life and the next,
no matter how we fare.

We swore to that, through our youth, manhood, and old age.
Hours and decades passed.
There were places and events remembered as we talked,
lingering there holding tight to yesterday, reluctant to turn the
    page.

* * *

Departing Lucca's, we wrapped our arms around each other,
sympathetic, comforting arms
linked through eternity,
man to man, brother to brother.

"So mote it be."

Tomorrow stretches out for those who still remain and weep,
With promises of progress and "miles to go before we sleep."
The circle's unbroken, for what we've sown is what we now shall
    reap
a love sown deep stays profound within us, trumping pain and
    grief.

* * *

Bois would have, most likely, termed this homage corny,
bluster, excessive verbiage, full of baloney.
He'd insist we make no fuss.
"After all, B, I was just an ordinary, ornery cuss."

I pray up there he's found great pleasure
as we bid him farewell with fondest measure,
while gathering in one of his chosen places,
to raise our drinks with tear-streaked faces.

The angels have made their claim.
With brotherly love and heavy hearts,
we whispered soft,
"All Honor to His Name."

for Jim Boisclair

Lover of Life

You were a lover of life.
A fact no one can deny.
New Year's Eve, Fourth of July,
homemade pie and Semper Fi.

Ours was an idyllic youth, full of escapades and fun.
Through barren fields and mowed backyards, carefree we would
    run.
We hurled some balls, chased girls in summer's lingering light,
swung for the short left-field fence with all our skinny might.

Lime dialed in his RCA, cheering for the hapless Cubs.
Evening came, and out we'd go with Bobby J and/or Eric Ubs.
We snuck out in the dark of night, negotiating tangled brush,
returning through morning dew—in a quiet hush.

You, Jungle Gym King of the Mountain at Silas Willard School,
strong, tough as a workhorse, a wily, stubborn mule.
You sent us tumbling down to cinders far below,
a terror then, but little did we know

what friends we'd soon become. As Streaks, Blue and Silver, our
    lives became a sprint.
Through thirteen curves in Mr. Ed, we'd spin without a dent. A car
    so cool, so hip, so mint!
The Beatles and the Stones rocked and rolled, they'd barely just
    begun,
later we sat in gowns and mortarboards, our high school days now
    done.

Venturing south, we departed to Bloomington, to good, old IWU.
Kappa was your library, a classroom just for you.
A place like Jake's—honest workingmen—like the ones you knew.
You said farewell to college days—to Pendleton you flew.

Back home you came in faded bibs, sweet Eube by your side.
Back home slightly changed, smitten by your bride.
Boys were born to you and Pam, your lovely wife;
a home on Broad—a raucous, joyous life.

Construction, in your blood, soon became your trade.
Projects galore, a brand-new home, all you somehow made.
But there remained a greater treasure, one you'd always sought,
beyond bricks and mortar or things that could be bought.

To be a friend to all,
to everyone you met.
A presence big, never small,
a man we'll not forget.

* * *

For sixty years our friendship grew,
dining, joking, celebrating, throwing back a Coors or two.
Reminiscing of games and days gone by,
laughing so hard we'd often cry.

We traveled thousands of miles with our favorite crew.
Danced the Electric Slide—which you could never do.
The Hens plus Cuffy, Hawk, Kelly, Bo.
Oh, the places we did go.

Never a dull moment with you,
after all, you knew more than Google knew.
Your stories, laugh, and smile always filled the room,
much like when you and Cuffy shot a double moon.

* * *

Your lessons remain, the ones you taught us, oh so well—
to love and never dwell
on sadness, pain or strife.
In sorrow now, we sit and muse—grateful for your life.

Semper Fi—be always faithful, always loyal—a motto you lived
    by every day.
A life so full of love and joy, it clearly lit the way.
If given the chance to speak today, maybe this is what you'd say:
"Love life as I did; smile, laugh, play, have fun, but don't forget to
    pray."

Live life to its fullest would be your reminder.
Be good to each other, gentler, sweeter, kinder.
We loved you, Roscoe Willie, a man so good and true.
We'll hug and love each other, you showed us what to do,

we'll laugh through our tomorrows, toss aside our burdens too,
we'll laugh through tears of gladness, as we remember you.

for Steve Fox

A Death in Venice

In Rome
we walked on cobblestone streets that predated Christ,
who was everywhere—
in paint, mosaics, and marble.

His birth and resurrection
chronicled in great detail
by artists
who had perfected their craft.

In Florence,
David stood tall and proud,
as we strolled amongst sculptures that reflected
centuries of cultural history and beauty.

* * *

You left us in Venice.
Boney, bowed, bird legs,
short shorts,
floppy Jungle Jim hat,

walked cautiously away with sweet Diane,
boarded a water taxi on the Grand Canal,
hoping to hydrate
in this city of water.

We waved to you.
And then in this land of romance, this land of saints,
with little warning,
you were gone.

In the hours following,
we witnessed unceasing love
from those angels
who knew you ever so briefly or even not at all.

And there was the strength of Di's love,
stretched across the decades
steeped in the moments
you'd shared.

Permeated by what happened
in a stark waiting room,
we were bound through our tears by a friendship
of authenticity, honesty, and truth.

* * *

As St. Mark's bells peal through the streets,
we survive with our sorrow.
Yours was a death in Venice, but your spirit
lives on; each act of your kindness, compassion,
    and generosity

was a small miracle that continues to sustain,
inspire, and remind all of us that you are now
in the presence of all the saints
that have gone before.

I am certain you are watching over us,
just as you always did.
The heroic knight, Sir Bo—loyal, loving,
unselfish, and never forgotten.

Your words came clearly to me in the middle of the night,
"Love on, love on, love on with all your might."

for Ed "Bo" Olds

Ascension

There is beauty in a moment
remembered, not forgotten.
A mid-August day—
the late-afternoon sun falling

into golden fields.
The wind whistling
through tassels
and thistles.

Grasses stretching
to the sky.
Ashes floating
through summer air.

Take off!
Fly away!

You—here in spirit.
You—here in our hearts.
Remembering moments,
not forgotten

rather etched
deep where
memories
dwell.

You left us
in Venice,
unexpected,
a much-too dramatic exit.

These remains,
spread here
today on ground
you considered hallowed,

are a mere
physical reminder of you.
For you are embedded in each
of our souls.

We will remember you
on this day, and all others,
until our flight
departs.

Until then
we pledge to
take it all in
doing our best

to appreciate
the moments
that remain.
To be grateful.

Your spirit still
lives within us,
as our love soars,
ascending

from our souls
to yours.

for Ed "Bo" Olds

Swimming Through Shadows

"Poetry is an echo, asking a shadow to dance."
CARL SANDBURG

Swimming in the lake
you so enjoyed,
lost in motion,
strokes, breath;

the sun
dipped behind the trees lining the coast.
The late-afternoon shadows
reminded me you were gone.

"Between the essence
and the descent
falls the Shadow,"
Eliot wrote.

You had, after all,
emerged from the shadows
years ago
and moved on.

Your essence
was never concerned
with descent (unless it was from a diving board
    into deep water),
but rather ascent.

That was the gift you gave
to those of us
you mentored
and loved.

You encouraged us
to soar,
to tell our own stories,
to be truthful to ourselves.

You were the finest type of teacher:
encouraging mentor,
constructive critic.
You refreshed our souls

with your authenticity,
your kindness,
your honesty,
your compassion.

You made everyone comfortable.
Authors, actors, sculptors, rock musicians,
aspiring writers, even awkward youth—
all succumbed to your Southern charm.

Ceaselessly you demonstrated how to be grateful
for family,
for friends,
and esteemed colleagues.

We trusted you
with our stories,
our lives,
and the stories and lives of those we loved.

From Sandburg and Wilder,
to Steichen and Jones,
you exposed us to greatness,
even as your own swimming lessons inspired
    and challenged us.

A shadow has fallen upon us
a pall descended over us,
but your spirit won't allow it.
You will have none of that.

The poem of your life
dances with the shadow.
It echoes throughout our lives
with no regret.

Your essence
neglected the notion of being even remotely hollow.
It was full.
You trusted the power whose center is everywhere.

That was how
you taught us to live.
That is how you would
want us to emerge from the shadow of our grief:

full of promise and bliss,
loving each moment
just like the saints and poets
and you.

for Penelope Niven

Glory Days

"Glory Days yeah they'll pass you by
Glory days in the wink of a young girl's eye
Glory days, glory days"

FROM "GLORY DAYS" BY BRUCE SPRINGSTEEN

You were one of my first heroes.
A consummate athlete
in three major sports—
elite.

You captured my imagination,
gave me a dream, a goal
to one day wear
a uniform of silver and gold.

Whether dashing across a goal line,
leading a "controlled" break—so sublime,
or smashing a line-drive single,
you made such an impression on me.

My dad was finally able
to purchase two season tickets.
We sat high up—row T,
cheering on you and the Streaks.

You skipped along, dribbling the ball,
distributing to Nixon, Cannon, Havens, Sandburg, et al.
Later, it was you and your running mate, Tucker.
You were one hard-nosed *competitor* (better keep this PG-13).

* * *

Back then, I never could have imagined
you would one day be my friend,
dodging my errant casts,
blowing skeet out of the air with a shotgun,

drinking morning coffee without a care,
reminiscing about the glory days
of playing games and coaching ways:
a State Championship, even knocking over a chair!

You were always quick with a story.
We had so many great times,
so many laughs,
even tears, especially when we lost Russ.

Later, life got even rougher,
but you stepped up,
and took care of lovely Alice.
Oh, how you could make her laugh.

I didn't observe that from row T,
but rather up close and personal
where I saw what a real hero you were,
and what a hero she also was.

Glory days may pass us by
in the wink of a young boy's eye,
but I believe, for all of us, the best
is yet to come. I know you believe that, too.

Thanks for always being you,
my hero—today and always.

for Gary Bruington

Across Miles and Years

Me, an English teacher? Laughable.
But the interview was actually affable—
Mr. Dennis, a wonderful man.
I answered his shocking f-word question truthfully—
    the only way I can.

There was honesty here, far beyond the pale,
amidst the green and gold;
a newer tale,
one day would be told.

I secured my keys;
not a person did I know.
From down the hall you and Bo
approached me,

stuck out your hands and offered friendship;
two fellas, also unknown,
but in that moment, there was a kinship,
forever, faithfully, sown.

A brotherhood born—
teachers, coaches; a sacred duty sworn.
We were also husbands—a vow devotedly taken,
our wives, our partners—lives shared in the future we
    were making.

I was a father, too.
A bit later that would come for both of you;
roles—fully embraced—through
and through.

Chopper, Mimi, Cornyns, Erdmans, et. al
joined our group.
Bo, the social chair, such a loyal pal;
gathered us together, forming a pithy, tight-knit troop.

We taught, coached, and partied;
pursued advanced degrees.
Trekking forth together, we set out to seize
the knowledge WIU had purportedly embodied.

Driving 'cross darkened roads,
through rain and ice and snow,
laughing, sharing histories—off to Macomb and the Quad-
	Cities we'd merrily go.
Trudging toward our common goals

to build a life of worth,
for family and our wives.
To forge ahead, to toil, to educate, to strive,
to make a better world, one of purpose, joy, and mirth.

Our friendship—steadfast and ever true,
much like your rocket arm at quarterback,
or from the outfield, where you threw
swift runners out—not a legend, just a fact.

You told us, "Let that dirty, ornery tackler through,"
as into his family jewels the football you then threw—*smack!*
The days of youth, oh, if we could only get them back;
days long gone by, replete with storied memories of our
	iconic crew.

* * *

Diaspora, the official term—
reality reared her ugly head, unforeseen in August's first few days.
You traveled away, 'cross far-reaching, long-sought highways.
Challenging lessons lay ahead, ones we'd all be forced to learn.

A few went north or east; you went west.
We who remained sat drenched in certain sorrow.
Suddenly, our friends departed reluctantly upon unchartered
    quests;
they soared, unknowingly, toward a promising new tomorrow.

Time and distance will never diminish
what had once been so thoughtfully wrought.
Our friendships, far from finished,
have created lifelong bonds, never sold or bought.

Once begun when we were young,
our affections have lasted long.
Through waning years,
we've shared our celebrations and also shared our tears.

We've laughed and cried,
from Lombard to London, and finally, to the Lake,
remembering times, long gone by,
but, oh, what memories we did gladly make!

Life's mysteries still abound,
answers yet unknown,
but this, for certain, is one thing I have found.
Through the years, we've matured and grown,

decades now have gently passed,
but a friendship like ours
continues, forged through years, miles and hours,
a friendship that will forever last.

You'll not be forgotten, my friend—always one of the best—
as long as forever is for me, I'll remember you—until my
    final breath.

for Fred Keeperman

The Sweet Soul

One would have to wonder,
was there ever a sweeter soul,
a kinder person
than you?

You seemed to perfectly understand
the rhythms of life.
never in much of hurry,
never flustered or even slightly worried.

There was a grace about you,
even in your dreadful illness.
You never complained
or spoke harshly of others.

Your kindness was pervasive;
it affected everyone around you,
all those you loved,
especially your daughter.

On top of everything, you laughed
at my silly jokes and sense of humor.
Then there was the time when you also
told me to grow up. (It was sound advice.)

You were generous and benevolent,
giving of your time and talents,
especially to your grandchildren,
who adored you.

You raised a daughter
who models today many of your fine traits;

industrious, elegant, self-sacrificing,
thoughtful (she still *writes* thank-you notes),
    and compassionate.

You once told her to "pass it on."
She has done so
with a high degree of competence
and kindness.

She is adored
by her children,
grandchildren,
and friends.

She was the ultimate professional
in her chosen field,
and saved the lives
of countless children.

I know you were proud of her
and the fine person she is.
Much of that can be attributed
to how she was raised.

Your life ended tragically—
an accident.
But we will always remember you
as the sweet soul you were.

You are locked
into the memory bones of our family
and serve as a lasting template
of a life well lived.

for Ida Dell Zumwalt

The Designer

Now I realize
where she gets it from,
her creative bent,
her need for symmetry.

Standing by your side,
observing your engineering skill,
when painting a wall
or building a boat,

she observed a master of craftsmanship
at work.
Was there anything you couldn't build
or figure out?

A doll house,
a tree house,
reflooring a garage attic
when you were eighty years old.

You set a high bar, my friend.
awash in honesty and integrity,
from councilman to 33rd degree,
you were a model to all.

You intimidated me,
struck the fear of God
into my skinny body,
but mutual respect eventually emerged.

You granted me permission to marry
the woman we both loved.
We gave you three gifts you cherished
as much as life itself—your grandchildren.

You gave me another priceless gift, too—
a treasure in a box,
the story of your brother,
and your family.

I came to better understand
the man you were,
upon learning you were
sent to the farm as a young boy.

Such an experience was precursor
to the man you would become—
driven, conservative, a patriot,
a man of unyielding principle.

From teacher to engineer,
you were admired by your peers,
even as you traveled abroad
to teach others what you knew.

Admired and venerated you retired,
reaping the rewards of your achievements.
Little did you know
what challenges you were about to face.

As always, you rose to the occasion,
even in the face of immense tragedy.
In your later years you mellowed
into a beloved grandfather and great-grandfather.

Whether walking the mall or traveling to visit loved ones,
you remained a model to emulate,
never seeming to age,
always ready with a joke or story.

On a lovely, peaceful, spring, Sunday morning you left us.
You'd prepared a prayer
to deliver at the church you loved,
the one where we would honor you one last time.

Your life was dedicated to hard work
and veracity.
You were loved by many, especially your family.
That is your legacy, the ultimate design you left to us.

for Homer Zumwalt

The Quiet Man

As the years pass,
I have grown
to appreciate you
even more.

There are days
I wish I was more like you—
kinder, less egomaniacal,
a better work ethic.

You tried to drill
that into me,
even while raking
ubiquitous leaves.

Who cared if they
were hiding
behind the shrubs?
You insisted on doing it right!

We played catch once—
no *Field of Dreams.*
And yet,
you were, and still are, my hero.

You didn't die like your brother, Bobby.
Sadly, there was a fragment
of survivor's guilt
laid at your feet by Grandma.

But you persevered.
You were a survivor,
a veteran, bound and determined
to make a better life, to make it count—

marry your soulmate,
raise good kids,
make a decent living,
be kind and fair-minded to others.

Your wounds weren't visible;
loss of your siblings,
especially your sister, Anna May,
would cripple most.

And then there was Grandpa,
gone too soon.
The war
had to be left behind.

And you did.

It's only now
I fully appreciate
the complete man
you were.

You did your best,
approached all of life's complexities
with a sense of humor
and sincerity.

Those who knew and worked with you
appreciated your disposition,
And, of course, your work ethic.
Down to the last, damnable leaf.

You displayed love every day.
I never completely
understood it,
but I felt it.

Your love was quiet, unassuming,
as the Bible says—patient and kind.
Now, I know not all fathers were like you.
Some were mean, demanding, violent, full of demons.

I sit here composing,
thankful I had you for my father.
I told you a few times,
in one fashion or another, but not enough.

These words
now, at last, memorialize
my remembrance of you—
the quiet man, my father.

for F. DeWayne Swanson

The Pragmatist

Pragmatist.
That's what you called yourself.
You sat there
in your blue upholstered rocking chair,

reminiscing about days gone by;
frustrated you couldn't remember
what you had for lunch
or which game you'd last watched,

afraid you would end up
being a burden.
There wasn't
the slightest chance of that.

You were seldom effusive
with praise,
mostly a backhanded,
secondhand compliment—

something someone else
had said about me,
still, I always knew
you loved me.

Later, when I had my own,
I understood it completely.
Such feeling resides
deep within—indescribable.

Just there.

And you were—
as nurse, friend,
aunt, sister, sister-in-law,
cousin, wife, mother.

Wisdom and nurture
bathed in practicality—
sensible, realistic,
reasonable.

I listened and took your advice
most of the time.
Later, I grew to appreciate
your innate intelligence.

Even in your twilight years
you read a book almost every day,
never missed a birthday,
anniversary, or noteworthy event—

sending a card
in your distinctive penmanship,
clear, concise, sincere—
just like you.

With elegance
you maintained your beauty,
inside and out.
It mattered to you.

You imbued
such attentiveness
to most of
your descendants.

The same with sustenance.
I remain stricken
with the tastes
rustled up in your kitchen.

You maintained you were a simple person.
You were not.
You were extraordinary
and that is what I will remember—always.

I am not a pragmatist.
I'm a dreamer.
You granted me permission for that
because you knew that is what I am.

For that, and so much more, I will
love you with eternal gratitude.

for Betty Ottoson Swanson

About the Author

Barry Lee Swanson is an author, poet, U.S. Army veteran, and Assistant Professor Emeritus from Knox College in Galesburg, Illinois. He received his B.A. in English literature from Illinois Wesleyan University and a master's degree in educational administration from Western Illinois University.

After a career in public education as an English teacher, coach, and school administrator, Swanson served as a full-time lecturer in the College of Education at the University of Illinois in Champaign-Urbana where he earned his Doctor of Education degree.

He is past president of the Carl Sandburg Historic Site Association and a founding member of the Galesburg Public Art Commission. His first novel, *Still Points*, received stellar reviews and is an Amazon Best Seller. He is currently writing his second novel.

Barry and his wife, Gail, reside on Lake Norman in North Carolina. They have three children and five grandchildren.

CPSIA information can be obtained
at www.ICGtesting.com
Printed in the USA
JSHW080717270423
40911JS00002B/111